LAMP Stack for Humans

How to turn a laptop into a web server on your local network

by Jay Versluis

First Edition
Version 1.2

ISBN: 151145749X
ISBN-13: 978-1511457491

TABLE OF CONTENTS

INTRODUCTION

THE TOOLS

ABOUT CENTOS

INSTALLING CENTOS AND LAMP PACKAGES

CONFIGURING YOUR LAMP STACK

COMMAND LINE CRASH COURSE

INSTALLING WEB APPLICATIONS

CONNECTING TO YOUR SERVER
FROM OTHER COMPUTERS

INSTALLING CENTOS 6 (32 BIT)

EXTRAS

ABOUT THE AUTHOR

Introduction

I was talking to a friend of mine the other day and explained how we use WordPress as a shared notebook for our internal office needs. Because we're dealing with confidential data, from credentials to staff training, we've decided not to host it "in the Cloud" and instead have it accessible only from our office network. It's cheaper and more secure that way.

Intrigued he could see the possibilities and asked, "Wow, it sounds difficult to setup - how did you do it?" Over a very long chat it transpired that a written guide would be handy, both for him, my colleagues, interested geek friends and many other souls who want to do the same thing: run a private web server, shielded from the rest of the world.

At first I considered a long blog post, but because the subject matter that needs to be discussed greatly varies from one topic to another, I thought perhaps a series of blog posts would be better. Even so, the main article would have contained many links to other articles, and if you want to just go through the whole process and set this thing up in one session, then a series of interconnected web articles is not the best way of working.

When I presented the idea to my wife she said, "Why don't you write a short book about this, so people can download it and read it at their own leisure? Besides, then we can all read it, with or without an Internet connection".

And so I did. Here you have it: the complete guide to turning an old computer into your personal Internet server. Rather than presenting the idea that "you can do everything with this setup" (which of course you can), I will stick to a very distinct procedure:

- Install CentOS (a very stable operating system)
- Install the LAMP stack (which is Linux, Apache, MySQL and PHP)
- Make the necessary tweaks to run WordPress on it
- Setup other devices to access your local WordPress instance via your Web Browser
- Include Mac and Windows PCs, as well as iOS and Android Devices
- And of course: daily backups so your data remains safe

Along the way I will explain - from one human to another - why we're doing what, and what we're doing step by step. There's nothing worse than some tech-speak that mere mortals don't understand. Rather than rattle down shell command, I will take you on a fascinating journey of taking an old laptop you have sitting in a corner and turning it into an always-on personal server.

The same principles of creating a LAMP stack on your local network also apply to servers and VMs hosted out there "in the Cloud" (i.e. publicly on the internet). You don't need to be a computer power user to follow my instructions, nor do you need any prior knowledge of Linux. If you do, it will of course help – but please don't feel patronised when I explain things in terms too simple for your taste.

All you need to bring is a willingness to learn and explore, a healthy interest in technology and software, and some experience in the web application of your choice. I will use WordPress as an example, because that's what we use in our office, but I will not go into much detail about using WordPress. Our focus will be to get that LAMP Stack up and running and ready for use.

Having said all that, let's begin!

JAY VERSLUIS, Miami Beach, FL

February 2015

What is a LAMP Stack?

Originally the acronym LAMP stood for Linux, Apache, MySQL and PHP. It describes a collection of open source software packages working together, stacked on top of each other so to speak. This stack is commonly used to power web based applications, which are nowadays just as powerful as the full-blown desktop applications we use. Such web applications can be built once and accessed from every platform and operating system that is capable enough to run a suitable web browser. WordPress, Facebook and Wikipedia are examples of such web applications.

The bottom layer of the LAMP Stack is the operating system: this is typically one of the many Linux distributions such as CentOS, Fedora, Debian, Ubuntu or any of the others. But because Linux is just the Kernel, it's not really an operating system - hence a LAMP Stack is often referred to as an AMP Stack.

On top of our Linux distribution run several system services called daemons, little programmes that are always on and waiting for requests. One of them is a web server, commonly Apache, responsible for serving static files to a requesting browser. Another one is the database server, commonly MySQL, which is used to store and retrieve table-based data from a data store.

But static files alone will make it very difficult to create a relevant query, which is why the stack also makes use of a programming language, commonly PHP. It can speak to MySQL and is served by Apache, and as such needs to be installed as an addition to the web server. PHP is a scripting language that is compiled at runtime and is executed on the server. The result of its output – thanks to the web server – is turned into HTML and other files on the fly, and the web browser at the receiving end displays the output, just as if it was a static website.

The first Linux Kernel was released in 1991, and Apache, MySQL and PHP were released around 1995. Together they were used for countless websites that today we call "web applications". The term was coined because of the amount of interactivity we can have with them, as opposed to surfing a static website.

In the early days of its inception, this innocent software stack lead to such an increase in business ideas on the web that only five years later the "internet bubble" burst around 2000. You could argue that the arrival of the LAMP Stack is a significant milestone in the history of the Internet.

Over the years, clever people have found replacements or amendments for each part of the LAMP Stack: instead of Apache, we could use another web server such as NGINX or lighttpd. Instead of MySQL we could use another database server, perhaps MariaDB or PostgreSQL. And instead of PHP we could use Ruby on Rails, PERL or Python.

Each of these changes can outperform the original technologies in specific situations, but because the role that each piece plays in the puzzle remains the same, the acronym LAMP stood the test of time.

It is possible to run a LAMP Stack on your local desktop computer using WAMP Server or XAMPP for Windows, or MAMP for macOS (a beta for Windows is underway). Such packages install Apache, MySQL and PHP along with a number of handy tools to get you started with simplified control options.

As long as you're the only member of your team to access locally installed web applications, these packages will work just fine - but if you want to give the rest of your team access to those applications, you'll run into a problem: your local computer is not always on, and not all of the above packages allow external access to your local web server from other machines on the network.

What this book is about

In this book I will show you how to set aside a separate computer that will take on the role of a server in your own network. Everyone who is part of that network will be able to access your web applications and start using them for collaborative work.

What you run on the LAMP Stack is completely up to you. I will show you how to install WordPress because we use it for collaborative work at the office in tandem with the P2 theme - but you can run anything you like, even several web applications at the same time: perhaps your own Wikipedia, or your private inter-office phpBB message board.

Who this book is for

You may be a power user who is happy on Windows or macOS, and you're heard of this "Linux thing". Perhaps you're curious, or maybe you want to start testing the waters before taking the concepts discussed here to the World Wide Web and a cloud instance. No prior knowledge of Linux or the LAMP Stack components is required, but it doesn't hurt if you know what HTML is.

You may have tried to follow 500-word Internet articles and ultimately have run into problems because although factually correct, random commands without context weren't enough to satisfy your hunger for the "knowledge of more". While I will show you all those commands, I will also explain why we need to use them so you can apply the principles to your own projects. I will also point you in the right direction if and when more details are available in the form of links.

All you really need is the desire to get your hands dirty with new software and the desire to learn. At least two computers and a local network are required to follow along, one of which can be an old device that hasn't seen much use lately – perhaps because it's too slow to keep up with the latest version of Windows.

As long as it's an Intel or AMD device with at least 512MB of RAM and a network connection you can use it: a LAMP Server isn't as power hungry as your average desktop computer, at least not when used by less than 100 concurrent users.

Formatting conventions in this book

Much of what we do with Linux happens on the command line. Hence I will frequently include code snippets and show you commands that need to be executed with an SSH client.

These are formatted in a different mono-spaced font and a dark grey background so they stand out from the rest of the text. Here's an example:

```
cd /Directory
```

I may also show you two commands that need to be executed on a row, and I will show those with one command per line:

```
cd ~/Downloads
ls
```

Some commands are executed silently, which means they do not generate any output. Others however will produce text that will be displayed in the same window. If that's the case, I will add this output underneath the command, separated by a space, like so:

```
uptime
```

```
13:41  up 47 mins, 4 users, load averages: 1.33
1.26 1.13
```

In the above example, I would expect you simply to type "uptime" and not the rest. You may see a lot of text output, and I don't want to frighten you off: this is not a "type-in adventure" (even though at times it will feel like it).

From time to time I may indicate a comment which is not part of the shell's output, nor is it meant to be typed in. For example, if an operation takes a long time to produce any output, I will use two forward slashes to indicate this:

```
command --long-calculation
// time passes...

shell output goes here
```

Having said all that, smaller e-book readers may try to break the lines in their own way, which can lead to very confusing code snippets. In the above example (uptime), there are exactly two lines of text. But if the second line does not fit on the e-book reader, then it is broken at a random point, leading to three lines.

If you're experiencing this problem, you can decrease the font on your device to something smaller to make these lines appear cohesive. Alternatively, it may help to put your device in landscape mode – at least until that the code snippet makes sense.

This is usually not a problem on larger devices, but I know from reading many e-books how inconvenient badly formatted code snippets can be. I've tried to make this experience as painless as possible for you.

And just one more thing: I will often refer to "other parts of this book" in which something related is explained in greater detail. I have done my best to include clickable links to such sections in this book.

To return to the main text after clicking and examining such sections, please use the back button (or option) on your device. It's not always easy to find. See if you can find it for even easier navigation.

The Tools

We need a variety of tools for our CentOS adventure:

- 1x dedicated server hardware (perhaps a laptop)
- 1x USB stick or card reader
- An Internet connection
- An SSH Client, such as PuTTY, Terminal, or Prompt
- Patience, a hot drink, and some uninterrupted time

Let me explain these things in a bit more detail and why we need them.

The Server

The server will be the computer we'll install CentOS on. Its role in our network will be to respond to requests from web browsers at any time, and hence it will be an always-on machine. A low powered old laptop will probably do a great job, anything with an Intel or AMD processor purchased around or after 2005 will work fine. Even models going back as far as around 2000 will probably work. We don't need a lot of processing power, RAM or even hard disk space for this little guy.

One component that will fail on any computer over the years is the hard drive. Spinning hard drives have always let moderately good hardware down and are responsible for making your computer operate slower than what it's capable of.

If you are using old hardware, I highly recommend investing into a new hard disk and replacing it before you start, especially because our server will become an always-on machine holding valuable data. We don't want it to stop working two weeks from now. SSDs are cheap these days and turn even old computers into very capable machines.

Laptops in particular make great candidates for our server project:

- laptops are easy to store and come by
- laptops have an integrated display and keyboard
- laptops have an integrated battery for backup power

An integrated battery means our data is protected even when our office suffers from a power outage. An integrated display and keyboard will function as a "local terminal", which makes both installation and troubleshooting very easy.

The Client

To talk to the server we also need a client. This is any computer that wishes to connect to our server. Whenever you browse a website on the Internet, your computer - or more accurately, your web browser - is the client, and the server is the place on which said website is hosted.

We're going to build the same system here, so you'll need at least one other client in addition to your server.

I may refer to the client as "your laptop", as I imagine that's what you're connecting to the server from. But the term here is interchangeable and really only means "the machine that you work from in your office" (the term "office" itself is not necessarily meant literally).

So in essence, you'll need two laptops: one will become your server, and the other is your client.

The client can also be a mobile device, as long as it's on the same network as your server.

The USB Stick

We need a USB stick to create an installation medium. We will use it to boot your server for the first time and start the installation. An SD card or equivalent may work too, depending on your hardware.

If your server has a DVD drive you can also burn your own disk and install CentOS from there. We need to be able to boot from this medium, so make sure your hardware can boot from whichever medium you choose. I'm mentioning this because some laptops cannot boot from an SD card, but most will let you boot from USB or of course a disk. If you place an SD card into a USB card reader, then your computer will see this as a USB device and will boot from it just fine.

Depending on the size of the image you decide to download, your medium needs to be big enough to hold that data. A CentOS ISO is anywhere between 200MB and 8GB. We'll discuss which option is right for your system later.

A quick note on the quality of USB sticks: it's tempting to grab something that's been gathering dust in your desk drawer for a few years. I have USB devices from 10 years ago, and while their size will be more than adequate for our purpose, the read/write speed will likely be very slow compared to today's standards.

Older USB Sticks will technically work fine for creating bootable media, but you will pay the price in the time it takes to install CentOS. A fast USB stick means you can finish the installation in less than half an hour, while a slow USB stick means the same process can take several hours.

Internet Connection

To download the installation media and subsequent packages for your server we need an Internet connection. But there's more to it than the initial download:

Our server will be part of our office network at all times, and it will be connected to the Internet for occasional updates. Hence our connection needs to be permanent and always-on going forward. You can choose either a wireless connection using your Wi-Fi/WLAN network, or a wired connection using an Ethernet cable.

Note that if you want to install CentOS 6, there are implications to a wireless connection over a wired connection. I'm discussing these in detail in the CentOS 6 chapter of this book.

If you're using CentOS 7 either connection will work fine with the minimal installation image.

Command Line Tools (SSH Client)

Linux is known for and primarily used with command line instructions, issued via Shell Commands. It's the scary black screen with lots of green text that hackers like to use.

It's often a tad off-putting to new users and those who have grown up with graphical user interfaces (such as Windows). Don't be scared though, using the command line is relatively simple once you get over the initial shock, and certain tasks are actually easier to initiate with a text-based command than in a graphical window.

To connect to our server using the command line, we need to use an **SSH Client**. SSH stands for Secure Shell: sometimes known as the CLI, think of the shell as the language we use to communicate with the operating system at the other end. It's "secure" because every keystroke we type, and every single character we receive back from the server is encrypted.

If you're using a Mac, or even a Linux machine, then you can use a build-in tool called **Terminal**. On OS X it lives in Applications - Utilities, but a simple Spotlight Search will bring it up too. If you're using Launchpad on the Mac, you can find the Terminal utility in the "other" folder. And don't worry if you don't like the initial layout: you can use CMD and plus/minus to increase or decrease the font, and change the colours too (under Preferences).

If you're using Windows you need to install such a command line tool. My favourite is **PuTTY** (http://www.putty.org) but there are several others you can use too. Note that this is not the same as the "Windows Power Shell" or the integrated "Windows Command Prompt": even though they look very similar, an SSH Client speaks a very different language to the Windows Shell!

You can even get SSH Clients for mobile devices: I like using **Prompt for iOS** by Panic, Inc. Android users may want to look into **JuiceSSH** or **Terminal Emulator.**

Note that I do not recommend installing a whole LAMP Stack from a mobile device unless you have a keyboard attached at all times. For quick tweaks or updates however it's a great tool to have handy.

About CentOS

While there are many Linux distributions, I will explain how we setup our server using CentOS.

In this chapter I will explain what CentOS is and why it's a good choice for our project.

Why CentOS?

The idea behind our server is to build a system that once setup, we don't have to worry about anymore. CentOS is an ideal distribution because it focuses on stability and long term support, rather than bleeding edge innovation.

CentOS is built from source files developed by Red Hat for their commercial Red Hat Enterprise Linux operating system (RHEL). It has a life cycle of 10 years from the time a new version is released.

Other distributions have a life cycle which is much shorter: Fedora for example release a new version every 18 months, and support for older versions is typically only 6 months. This poses a problem because you risk that a new version may partly break the functionality of your server. And if that's not the case, you'll have to invest a lot of time making sure your server is updated regularly.

As a comparison, Ubuntu's LTS releases offer 5 years of support from the time of release, while Debian offers a maximum of 2 years. I will talk more about these two and other distributions in the Extras chapter of this book.

What is CentOS?

Before we start downloading CentOS, it's important to understand what it is and where it comes from.

CentOS is a Linux Distribution. It is free software, and - like the Linux Kernel - it can be re-distributed and amended by anyone who wishes to do so. You do not need a license key or anything similar to use it, you do not need to register with anyone, and you do not need to tell anyone that you're using CentOS. This is somewhat different when compared to Windows and macOS.

While the Linux Kernel is a very important part of an operating system, it does not work on its own. Other parts are needed to turn it into an operating system we can run on a computer. While we do have access to the source code, commoners like me wouldn't really know what to do with it to make my computer "go".

But more knowledgeable people do, and they are kind enough to compile those source files, along with many other useful bits and pieces which create something you and I can take and install on a computer - as we're about to do here.

The CentOS Project is a group of such knowledgeable people.

CentOS stands for Community ENTerprise Operating System and it's the third most popular Linux distribution powering today's web servers on the world wide web (the other two popular ones are Ubuntu and Debian).

The source files for CentOS are developed by Red Hat, a company that releases an operating system called Red Hat Enterprise Linux (or RHEL for short). This is a commercial product and binaries are not released, however the source code is. The CentOS Project take this very source code, remove any references to Red Hat (such as links, branding and images), and then release it as CentOS.

That explains why CentOS and RHEL are 100% compatible.

The CentOS Project is sponsored by Red Hat, who also own and sponsor the **Fedora Project**, makers of another Linux distribution by the same name.

Fedora's mantra is almost the opposite of CentOS: instead of long term package support and stability, Fedora strives to be very cutting edge and includes the very latest available packages into their distributions and release new versions very quickly (every 18 months). This incubates innovation, and it's great for experimental desktop projects – but less useful for servers like ours.

I'm mentioning this because any version of RHEL (and therefore CentOS) is based on a Fedora release that was frozen in time and branched off. While Fedora can continue to be innovative and move on to a new version, RHEL and CentOS can develop stable versions from such frozen branches.

At the time of writing, the current Fedora release is Fedora 22. For comparison, CentOS 6 was branched from Fedora 12/13, while CentOS 7 was branched from Fedora 19.

About Packages

I've been mentioning the term "package" for a while now without explaining what this means. It's only fair that I do before we delve deeper into the matter.

Every Linux distribution can be extended with other bits of software, usually from open sources. While it is possible to access the source code, it's not always a convenient way to bring this code into an operating system: it needs to be compiled and configured before it can be used. Other tools and yet more knowledge is needed to make this happen.

This is where packages come in: most software we need has already been compiled and is ready to be installed using packages. A package manager lets us find and add such software to our operating system.

In other words, a package is a compiled binary version of the software.

We'll learn how to install packages very soon, and we will use this technique extensively when adding every component our LAMP Stack needs to operate.

Hardware Requirements

CentOS 6 doesn't ask for a lot be happy: a modest 512MB or RAM and as little as 4GB or hard disk space can work fine. For CentOS 7, the minimum hardware recommendations are 1GB of RAM and at least 10GB of free disk space.

While older hardware may work just fine, especially for testing purposes, you need to consider if your server is to be a "hobby project" or a serious office tool: while it may not be a problem if a hobby project breaks down due to hardware age and incurs some serious data loss, the exact opposite is true for an office server which holds valuable data.

I will consider our project the latter and therefore recommend that you use quality components if your system is to be kept alive 24/7.

Determining
the right download

Before you begin downloading CentOS, you have an important decision to make: which version to download. This sounds easy, but your choice has implications that I will discuss here.

I'll make it as painless as possible, because in the world of Linux, everything is possible and there's a lot of choice. I don't want to bamboozle you with a plethora of possibilities and instead present only three choices:

In principle, you need to pick

- a major CentOS release (CentOS 7 and CentOS 6 are the current ones)
- an architecture (64 or 32-bit)
- an ISO type (minimal vs. full DVD image)

It depends on both your hardware and the physical placement of your machine:

If your hardware can run CentOS 7, you can use the **minimal ISO image**. Both a wired and a wireless connection can be setup during the installation. Additional packages we need can be downloaded after the initial setup. Note that CentOS 7 is only available for 64 bit processors.

If however your hardware is not capable of running a 64-bit operating system, you must run the 32-bit version of CentOS 6. And because it's easier to connect to a Wi-Fi network in CentOS 6 using a graphical user interface (GNOME), you should download the **full DVD image**. I will cover how to do this in the CentOS 6 section of this book.

I will explain how you can find out if your processor is 64-bit capable in the next chapter.

As a rule of thumb, and when in doubt, the 32-bit version of CentOS 6 will work on any hardware - even 64 bit capable hardware.

Is your CPU 64-bit compatible?

To see if your system can run 64-bit operating systems, you need to know your exact processor type. "Intel i7" is not enough; you need the model name string, which is something like "Intel i7-3615QM".

Here's how to find out how to do this on Windows, Mac and Linux.

Windows

On Windows, open the Command Prompt (under Accessories) and execute the **wmic** command with the following parameters:

```
wmic cpu get name

Name
Intel(R) Core(TM) i7-3615QM CPU @ 2.30GHz
```

Windows also gives you an accurate result via the GUI: open Windows Explorer and head over to Computer – Properties:

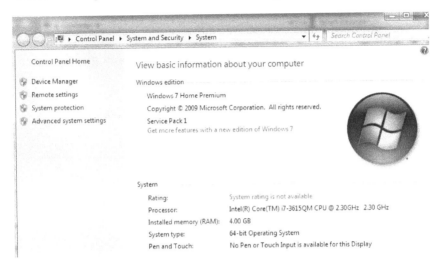

Mac

On the Mac you won't get a very accurate result from the "About this Mac" option that appears when you click the Apple icon. It will tell you what CPU type you're using, but not the exact model number.

Instead, open the Terminal utility (under Applications - Utilities, or search for it in Spotlight) and enter the following command:

```
sysctl -n machdep.cpu.brand_string

Intel(R) Core(TM) i7-3615QM CPU @ 2.30GHz
```

Linux

On any Linux distribution you can take a look at the **/proc/cpuinfo** file which holds a plethora of information about your system's CPU. So much in fact that it's difficult to find what you're looking for.

Filtering the output of this file for 'model name' gives you an exact match:

```
cat /proc/cpuinfo | grep 'model name'

model name : Intel(R) Atom(TM) CPU N270   @
1.60GHz
```

Researching your CPU

Now that we know the processor type, where do we go for further information on this CPU? As always, Google is your friend, but there are also two dedicated tools provided by Intel and AMD that may also be of help. Intel's ARK website is particularly helpful:

- http://ark.intel.com
- http://products.amd.com/en-us/

Look for something called instruction set, which will show you if your processor can understand 64-bit instructions.

You may find that you have a CPU that is neither Intel nor AMD, for example an ARM based one, or a Power PC. If that is the case, I'm sorry to say that you won't be able to install CentOS: it only works on i386 or x86_64 architectures.

Samsung Chromebooks for example run Exynos processors, which are indeed ARM CPUs. Non-Intel Macs (built prior to 2006) are Power PC based. You may still be able to install other Linux distributions, such as Fedora or Debian, but sadly not CentOS.

Downloading CentOS 7

It's time to start downloading CentOS, and the files we need come as ISO disk images. Several utilities can be used to transfer those onto bootable media, including USB sticks.

These ISO images are not hosted in a central place, but instead rely on mirror servers from which we can download them. Since CentOS is free, the project relies on sponsors who donate servers and bandwidth in several hundred locations across the globe. These mirrors are synchronised from the central CentOS server several times a day.

You can find the latest CentOS downloads at the following location:

http://www.centos.org/download/

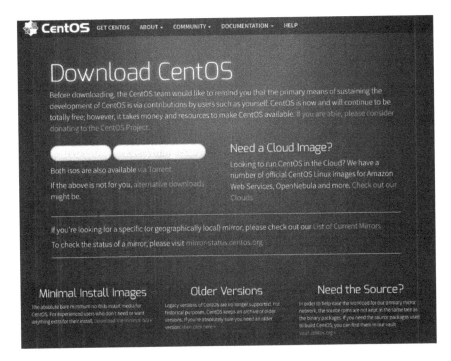

You will be directed to the latest version of CentOS and a list of direct links to the mirrors closest to you will be shown. You'll have a choice between DVD ISO, Everything ISO and Minimal Install Images (bottom left). The difference between these versions is that

- The DVD ISO fits onto a 4.7GB DVD, but may not include every single core package available.
- The Everything ISO includes every available package, but as a result is much larger (just under 8GB). The advantage is that you will not need an internet connection to install other core packages.
- The **Minimal Install Image** is under 400MB and includes only the bare necessities for running a CentOS system.

For our purposes the Minimal Install image is what we need, but feel free to download the Everything ISO if you have the time and patience.

Downloading CentOS 6

Even though it's still in use and supported for many years to come, CentOS 6 is already classed as an "older version". Substantial changes have been made in CentOS 7 and several system services differ - hence the team do not recommend downloading legacy versions.

But if you need to run a 32-bit version, or if you want to make use of the extensive documentation that has amassed on the web and in bookstores over the years, CentOS 6 is still a great operating system.

The direct link to this special section is http://wiki.centos.org/Download

Just in case the above link is no longer working, you can usually find a reference to "older versions" at the bottom of the CentOS download page at http://www.centos.org/download/

You should see a list similar to the one on the next page. On the left of the table you see the CentOS Version Number, next to which the latest minor release. Now take a look at the column labelled CD and DVD ISO Images. You'll see two sections here:

- i386 holds the 32-bit versions
- x86_64 holds the 64-bit versions

Select the **CentOS 6 / i386** link and you'll see a rather plain list of mirrors closest to you. Pick a mirror you like and you'll be directed to another rather plain list of links containing several files.

Download the one that ends in **DVD1.iso** with a simple click. The file is around 4GB in size and includes GNOME so we can connect to a wireless network as described in the CentOS 6 section.

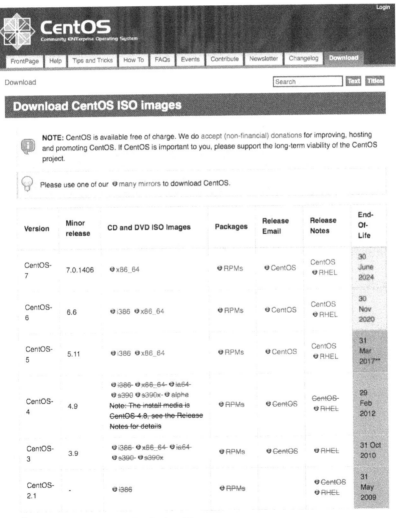

CentOS End-Of-Life

At the time of writing, CentOS 7 is the latest version of the project. It was released in July 2014 and will receive maintenance updates until June 2024.

The previous version was CentOS 6 and it's still widely used. It was released in July 2011 and will receive maintenance updates until November 2020.

CentOS versions cannot be upgraded in place, so you can't upgrade from CentOS 6 to CentOS 7 on the same machine, retaining most of your settings, like you can with Windows or macOS.

Tests to add such functionality to CentOS are underway, but it's a work in progress at the time of writing. What you choose now will be yours forever.

Transferring your ISO image to a USB Stick

It's good practice to verify the download you're about to transfer to your stick. It's not an essential step and rather technical, hence I've added an explanation in <u>the Extras chapter of this book</u>. For now we'll assume that your download has finished fine.

Instructions on how to transfer the ISO to your USB stick are different depending on the platform you're using to do this. Feel free to skip over what you don't need in this section.

You can of course transfer an ISO image to a DVD if your server has a DVD drive. The installation may take a fraction longer, but it's not worth worrying about. Most DVD burning software has the ability to transfer ISO images to DVD. Feel free to do this instead of the USB stick procedure.

Windows

A small utility called ISO2USB is available for all versions of Windows. It's one of the best tools I know to get the job done. It was specifically written to transfer CentOS and Red Hat Linux

45

ISO images to USB. You can download this tool here:
http://www.nirsoft.net/utils/product_cd_key_viewer.html

It couldn't be simpler to use:

- insert your USB stick
- start ISO2USB
- choose your ISO image
- hit run and relax

As soon as the tool finishes you can boot your server from this USB stick and start the installation.

macOS

On Yosemite and Mavericks we need to use a command line tool to transfer the image. The built-in Disk Utility will happily burn a DVD from our ISO image, but it refuses to create a bootable USB device. If your hardware allows it, I recommend burning a DVD.

Sadly the command line tool makes this step much more technical than it needs to be: it requires us to be comfortable with changing directories and issue commands and deal with Linux devices. I will explain it all, but right now is not the best time. Instead I will explain it all in a dedicated chapter in the Extras section of this book.

For the curious: There is an open source tool called UNetbootin which claims to be compatible with Mac, as well as Windows and Linux. I must admit that this tool has not worked for me on the occasions I've tried it – perhaps you are blessed with better luck:

- http://unetbootin.sourceforge.net

Installing CentOS and LAMP Packages

Finally, and with all the prep-work out of the way, let's take that installation medium and install it onto your new server. Either insert your DVD or plug in your USB stick, switch on your system and make sure it boots from an external device.

How to do this depends on the hardware you're using. It usually involves pressing a special key during the boot sequence. Sometimes a BIOS value needs to be set so that the boot sequence includes a USB or DVD drive, in addition to the internal hard drive. You probably know your hardware better than I do. If not, the manual that came with your machine will be able to help.

The installation for CentOS 7 and CentOS 6 greatly differs. Because both versions are good choices for our LAMP Stack, I've decided to show you both. In this chapter I will show you how to install CentOS 7. I've provided the same instructions for CentOS 6 in a later chapter of this book.

While it is possible to install CentOS alongside an existing operating system (such as Windows) I will not cover this procedure here. Instead we will format your server's hard disk, and as a result all data contained on it will be lost. In case you need anything, **now is the time to make a backup of your existing data before we proceed.**

After the installation, please keep your USB stick in a safe place. It will allow you to access your system in case of trouble and repair it.

Installing CentOS 7

The first screen you'll see is a rather simple text menu asking if you'd like to install CentOS or Troubleshoot. There's also an option that lets you test the installation media before installation. Choose the **first** option and continue.

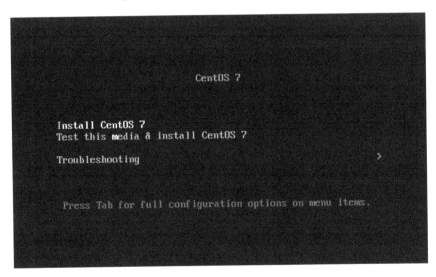

Next up is the language and keyboard selection screen. Pick as appropriate for your circumstances and hit continue at the bottom right.

From now on we'll be able to select items from the graphical user interface.

The following screen is the **Installation Summary**. It's an important one and has been greatly condensed in CentOS 7 compared with previous versions. Take your time here, there's a lot to choose from which will impact on how the system behaves when we come to setup the other components of our LAMP Stack.

As pictured, you'll see three sections here. You will return to this screen when you're done tweaking settings in any of the following three sections:

Under **Localization** you can customise your keyboard layout, language and the time zone you live in. You can also choose to let CentOS synchronise your local time via the internet, but because we haven't connected to it yet, this option won't be available. Feel free to come back when we've completed the section further down.

Under **Software** you can pick which source you'd like to install CentOS from. The default is Local Media, which is what we're using. To the right of it, under Software, the default is Minimal Install - which is perfect for our LAMP Stack.

Now let's deal with that orange explanation mark in the **System** section. Select Installation Destination and see a list of hard disks connected to your system. For laptops this is usually only a single drive, which is preselected at the top under Local Standard Disks.

In the likely event that your server already had a non-Linux system installed, you will receive a warning that there's not enough space left on the drive to install CentOS. When you get such a warning, select **Reclaim Disk Space** and you'll be presented with a screen like this:

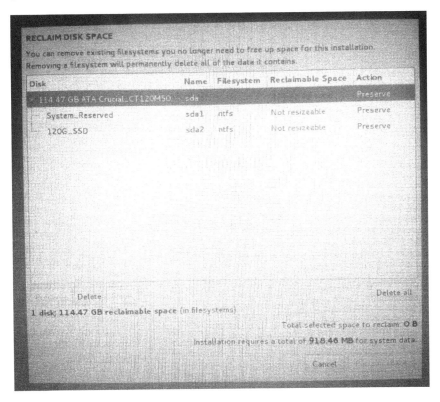

In the above example Windows 7 was already installed on our drive. To let CentOS remove both partitions, select the actual drive at the top (sda in my case) and click **Delete All**, followed by **Reclaim Space**.

We're finished with this section, so click Done and you'll find yourself back at the Installation Summary screen.

Now the orange icon disappears, and the previously greyed out **Begin Installation** button at the bottom right is now available. Don't click it yet though, we still need to setup your network connection.

Select **Network and Hostname**. It currently reads "not connected" and we're about to change this. On the left hand side you'll see a list of available network interfaces. Most computers have two interfaces, one for a wired connection, and one for a wireless connection. Exact results depend on your hardware.

Pick the interface that will connect your machine to your local network, be that wired or wireless, then flick the "on" switch on the right hand side. For wired connections, make sure the network cable is attached to your system. For wireless connections, select your network from the drop down menu and enter your Wi-Fi password when prompted. Wait a moment while CentOS determines your IP address and make a note of it - we'll need it for later.

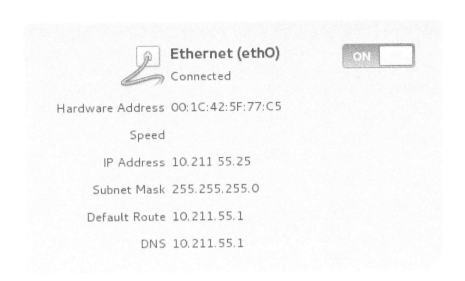

Ethernet (eth0)
Connected

Hardware Address 00:1C:42:5F:77:C5

Speed

IP Address 10.211 55.25

Subnet Mask 255.255.255.0

Default Route 10.211.55.1

DNS 10.211.55.1

Before we leave this screen, take a look at the bottom left box entitled **Hostname**. Currently it reads localhost.localdomain. That's the default name for your new server and it's not very creative or informative if you ask me, especially if you have more than one "localhost" on your network.

Rename it to something that describes your machine here. Rather than "server", call it something that reflects what the machine will be used for. Perhaps "linuxbox" or "centos".

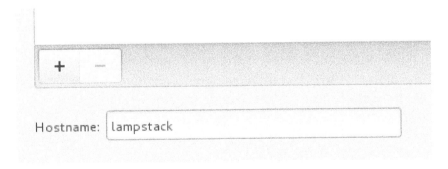

Hostname: lampstack

For our demonstration I'll call mine "lampstack", but anything goes here - from your pet's name to your company's name. When we connect to our server via SSH later, the hostname will be displayed after the username at the command prompt (like root@lampstack).

Make a note of your server's name (together with the IP address) and click Done at the top left. This should bring you back to the Installation Summary. Select **Begin Installation** at the bottom right to continue.

USER SETTINGS

ROOT PASSWORD
Root password is not set

USER CREATION
No user will be created

While CentOS is busy copying packages, a new screen will appear, entitled **Configuration**. You'll see two orange explanation marks asking you for user credentials. The first option (root password) will define your administrator password, and the second (user creation) will define credentials for a standard user. Here's why it is recommended to have two new users on your server:

Linux systems are multiuser environments, and root is the most powerful user in the hierarchy. root has read/write access to every file on the system and is only to be used for administrative purposes.

Due to the danger an accidentally mistyped command can bring, it is recommended to have an additional "standard user" for day-to-day tasks. This standard user can also be used for occasional administrative tasks (such as software updates and package installations), in which case we can give it administrator privileges too. This doesn't make it root though: instead the standard user needs to enter root's password if and when necessary. This saves having to logout and log back in again as someone else. macOS and Windows have more or less the same philosophy.

Having a standard user in addition to root is not strictly necessary for our setup, but since it's good practice I recommend to set one up anyway. Note that the installation will continue even if you only specify the root password without creating a standard user.

We can give the new standard user any name of our choice, but we cannot change the name of root. It will always be root.

Let's create our own user first by selecting **user creation**.

Fill in your full name, password and your desired user name. By default this is your own name without spaces in all lower case, but you can change it to something shorter (such as "me" - so your command prompt later would read me@lampstack). Give yourself administrator privileges by checking the tick box, then click Done to go back to the previous screen.

Now select the **root password** section and give root a nice strong password. Include cAptIaL LetteRs, numbers and special characters to make it as strong as possible. The slider will give us an indication as to how secure the password is. Make a note of it and click Done.

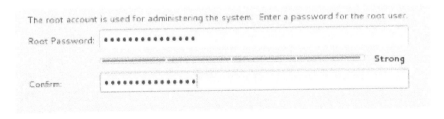

Wait for the progress bar at the bottom to finish and select **Finish Configuration** when your system is ready. This will be followed

by some more behind the scenes tasks, and as soon as CentOS is finished with those it will present you with a **Reboot** button to click.

Congratulations, you've just installed CentOS 7!

That's the first letter in our pursuit of creating a LAMP Stack: L for Linux. Now we can configure our server and put it to good use by installing the other three items we need: Apache, MySQL and PHP.

Speaking to CentOS

When your system starts up it will eventually come to the screen above, waiting for you to login. This may be very unfamiliar to folks who haven't used a minimal installation of a Linux distribution before. Since we're using our server as a remote system and won't access it locally that's just fine - we don't need a graphical user interface.

It's important to understand that you can login either with your own username and password (as setup previously), or as root, using the root password you've setup earlier.

It's also important to know that you can either login directly at the server, or login remotely using an **SSH Client**, if the computer you're logging in from is on the same network as your server.

The great thing about such a workflow is that your server can sit in a different part of the building, away from your desk, awkwardly stored and difficult to access. It doesn't even have to have a permanent keyboard or monitor attached. Thanks to your SSH Client you don't have to move from your desk if maintenance or system configurations are necessary on your server.

Let's login as **root** now because we need to do some additional setup to turn our server into a LAMP stack.

You can login with your own user name instead of root, but when you do you must execute administrative commands by prefixing them with the word **sudo**. This will give you temporary access to root privileges, requiring the root password with each command. In the following chapters I will assume that you are root already and will omit the sudo command from each line.

If you are at the server's local terminal, simply type root and the system will ask for your password.

If you're using an SSH Client (like I will) then you need to provide the IP for the server you want to login to. Type the following, replacing the IP address with your own:

```
ssh root@10.0.1.57
```

This will prompt for your password and will log you into the system. Now you'll see another prompt, waiting for your first command:

```
Last login: Wed Feb 18 17:05:07 2015 from
10.211.55.2
[root@lampstack ~]#
```

Should you experience trouble when logging in via SSH, check the Extras chapter of this book for possible solutions.

The command line is a powerful tool, and we'll use it a lot in the following chapters. I won't teach you every intricate detail about it in this book, but I will introduce several commands that are necessary to setup our LAMP Stack.

If you would like to delve deeper and learn more about the command line, I highly recommend William Shott's excellent book "The Linux Command Line":

- http://linuxcommand.org.

Updating Packages

Now that we're logged in to the system, let's install a few packages. Those are pre-compiled small pieces of software that can extend a barebones operating system like the one we have right now.

Installing packages on CentOS follows a simple pattern for which we use a command called **yum**. We'll make extensive use of it here, and we'll use it again from time to time to keep our server up to date. In a nutshell, yum can install, uninstall and update packages if a newer version is available. yum will also install related packages if they are needed for a package we want to use.

Let's start by updating our new server. It's likely that there have been several updates to the operating system since the ISO image we've used has been compiled. To check for updates, type the following:

```
yum update
```

yum will go to work and show you a list of available updates, or a message that no updates are available. Since this is the first time you're using yum it may take a moment or two. It'll be much faster on subsequent updates. Here's an excerpt of my output (it was a much longer list):

```
Loaded plugins: fastestmirror
base
| 3.6 kB  00:00:00
extras
| 3.4 kB  00:00:00
updates
| 3.4 kB  00:00:00
updates/7/x86_64/primary_db
| 6.6 MB  00:04:05
Determining fastest mirrors
 * base: ftp.usf.edu
 * extras: mirror.us.leaseweb.net
 * updates: mirrors.advancedhosters.com
Resolving Dependencies
--> Running transaction check
---> Package bash.x86_64 0:4.2.45-5.el7 will be
updated
---> Package bash.x86_64 0:4.2.45-5.el7_0.4 will
be an update
---> Package bind-libs-lite.x86_64 32:9.9.4-
14.el7 will be updated
---> Package libgcc.x86_64 0:4.8.2-16.el7 will
be updated
---> Package libgcc.x86_64 0:4.8.2-16.2.el7_0
will be an update
---> Package systemd.x86_64 0:208-11.el7 will be
updated
---> Package systemd.x86_64 0:208-11.el7_0.6
will be an update
--> Finished Dependency Resolution
Dependencies Resolved
=================================================
=
 Package                           Arch
Version
Repository     Size
```

```
======================================================
=
Installing:
 kernel                                  x86_64
3.10.0-123.20.1.el7
updates        29 M
Updating:
 bash                                    x86_64
4.2.45-5.el7_0.4
updates         1.0 M
 bind-libs-lite                          x86_64
32:9.9.4-14.el7_0.1
updates        711 k
 bind-license                            noarch
32:9.9.4-14.el7_0.1
updates         79 k
Transaction Summary
========================
Install   1 Package
Upgrade  79 Packages
Total download size: 95 M
Is this ok [y/d/N]:
```

Your list will be made up of all available updates for your system.
Enter **y** to proceed, or n if you'd rather not install these packages
right now. If you go ahead, yum will download, install and verify
all packages. It may occasionally stop and ask for your input, in
which case type y again until the installation has finished.

Instead of yum update, you could have also typed

```
yum -y update
```

which would check and install packages without the need for
further user input. That's a good option if you're in a hurry and
trust that all updates will be installed without problems (aka "the
Windows approach"), or if you'd like to run an update

62

automatically on a schedule. We will learn how to do this when we discuss automated backups later in this book.

When yum has finished it will return you to the command prompt with a friendly "Complete!" message.

Should you receive error messages instead, it is likely that your server is not connected to the internet. Rather than troubleshoot the problem, and because it's early days in our setup, start the installation process again and make sure you have a working network connection in the Network and Hostname section.

You can verify that you are connected to the internet by pinging a popular service such as Google or Amazon with the following command:

```
ping google.com
```

If your server is connected to the internet, you will receive a new line with Google's IP address every second. Press CTRL+C to stop the ping command.

If your server is not connected to the internet, you'll get a single line stating that you "Cannot resolve google.com: unknown host".

Switching off the Firewall

CentOS comes with a powerful firewall preinstalled. It's enabled by default and blocks all evildoers from accessing the server. Only SSH connections are allowed at this point so that we can configure the server, but all other connections are dropped automatically.

We will configure the firewall at a later point, but before we get into this, it's easier to switch it off for now. That way we can configure all other aspects of our LAMP Stack and enable the firewall when we come to configure it properly.

CentOS 7 has changed the service that is in control of the firewall. It's now called **firewalld**. In previous versions of CentOS (6 and earlier) this was handled by a service called **iptables**. Those are not the same, and applying syntax from one service won't work in the other.

To switch off the firewall on CentOS 7, type the following:

```
service firewalld stop
systemctl stop firewalld.service
```

To switch off the firewall on CentOS 6, use the following command:

```
service iptables stop
chkconfig iptables off
```

We will switch our firewall on again when we're ready to configure the service in a later chapter of this book.

Installing Apache

The A in LAMP Stack stands for Apache. This is our web server. Once installed, activated and configured, it will react to web requests and return data to a web browser, usually in the form of HTML and image files.

In a nutshell, when a request for http://yourserver/testfile.html comes in, Apache goes to work, looks for the file and returns it to the browser - which in turn displays its content.

By the way, these "always-on" services that run on your server in the background are called daemons, which is why many of them end in the letter d (as in firewalld). Apache runs as a daemon called **httpd**, probably because it deals with http requests. So if you hear people refer to "your web server", "httpd" or "Apache", they usually mean the same thing. Note that Apache is not the only web server in use today, but it certainly is the most popular and widespread one: Apache was used by 60% of all websites served on the internet in 2014. Just thought I'd mention it.

Let's install Apache with this simple command:

```
yum install httpd
```

This is a great example of how yum works: it knows that we really only need the httpd package, but it also knows that this package cannot work when installed just by itself. It needs other packages to fully function. Those are known as dependencies. yum is nice enough to install these dependencies for us and will let us know which ones they are.

Hit y to proceed. After a few moments, both Apache and whatever else is needed will be installed on your server.

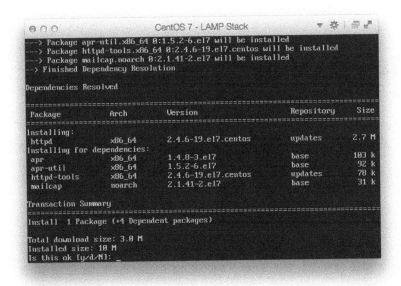

Starting Apache

Right now our web server is installed but it's not active yet. Let's start it with the following command:

```
systemctl start httpd.service
```

You will receive no output if the operation was successful. It would be cumbersome if we had to start the web server manually every time the server starts up. This is true for every service we want to use at all times. Therefore, let's make sure Apache starts as soon as the system has booted:

```
systemctl enable httpd.service
```

If all went well, Apache should produce some test output to indicate that it's working.

Let's try it out: open your favourite web browser and type in http:// followed by the IP address of your server (for example, http://12.34.56.78). You should be greeted by a friendly Apache Test page.

Testing 123..

This page is used to test the proper operation of the Apache HTTP server after it has been installed. If you can read this page it means that this site is working properly. This server is powered by CentOS.

Just visiting?

The website you just visited is either experiencing problems or is undergoing routine maintenance.

If you would like to let the administrators of this website know that you've seen this page instead of the page you expected, you should send them e-mail. In general, mail sent to the name "webmaster" and directed to the website's domain should reach the appropriate person.

Are you the Administrator?

You should add your website content to the directory /var/www/html/.

To prevent this page from ever being used, follow the instructions in the file /etc/httpd/conf.d/welcome.conf.

Promoting Apache and CentOS

You are free to use the images below on Apache and CentOS Linux powered HTTP servers. Thanks for using Apache and CentOS!

Your first ever website! Go celebrate!

So far so good - we have a basic working web server running. We will return to Apache later and make some configuration tweaks so that WordPress and other web applications can work with it using rewrite rules.

Installing MariaDB (MySQL)

The M in LAMP Stack traditionally stood for MySQL and describes our database server. While the web server can return static files, the database server can return data based on queries, typically text.

Web applications can ask things like "show me all entries from January" or "show me all posts from a certain category". Likewise, it's fast and easy for the database server to store text-based data (and sometimes even binaries), as well as create and query relationships between entries. Such a setup allows the front page of a website to serve the same layout with different content whenever a new post has been made available - all without changes to the static HTML files.

MariaDB vs MySQL

The MariaDB/MySQL relationship can be slightly confusion, thanks to political reasons. Here's a bit of background information on this subject:

The MySQL codebase was traditionally open source and released under the GPL license, just the like rest of our LAMP Stack. However, the company that created our beloved database server

(MySQL AB) was acquired by Sun Microsystems in 2008, which in turn was acquired by Oracle in 2009.

Since then, MySQL is still released as open source, but an open community is no longer involved in its development. Instead, Oracle write MySQL code in-house, behind closed doors, and release the source code when they deem it ready. In addition, Oracle has a major commercial competing database product, which makes some believe that support for MySQL may be discontinued in the future.

For these reasons, a lead developer of MySQL started a GPL fork of the project called **MariaDB**, aiming to be 100% compatible with MySQL. MariaDB is not under the pressures of the new management, and is considered a standalone GPL project that is "purely open source" again.

With the release of CentOS 7 the decision was made to support MariaDB instead of MySQL, which was supported up until CentOS 6. Because we're using CentOS 7, we need to install **MariaDB.**

For our LAMP Stack's functionality it isn't really important which version we run because every query generated by our web applications will work fine with either MySQL or MariaDB. The syntax and purpose of either version is the same as far as our LAMP Stack is concerned.

To install our database server, let's utilise yum again. In this case we need to install more than one package though, and we'll do this by simply separating each with a space:

```
yum install mariadb mariadb-server
```

The reason we need both packages is that on one hand, we'd like a MariaDB daemon to run that can serve and store data (mariadb-server). At the same time, we need to be able to interact with the server from a MariaDB client (mariadb) so that we can create a database and a user account for our web applications. These two packages rely on many others, a total of 9 dependencies and 108MB of downloads on my system:

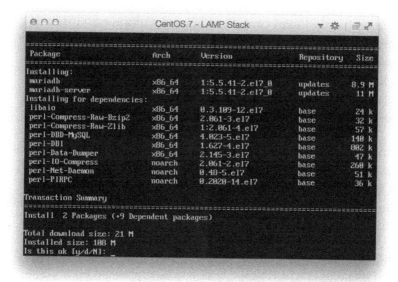

Starting MariaDB

Much like our web server, we need to start our database server:

```
systemctl start mariadb.service
```

And just like before, we would like MariaDB to start automatically when we reboot the server:

```
systemctl enable mariadb.service
```

Installing PHP

The P in our LAMP Stack stands for PHP. It's a scripting language that is used together with our web server. Web applications use it to make intelligent programming decisions based on several factors, many of which are saved as values in a database.

With PHP the website can be made to look different depending on factors such as "is the user logged in or not", "what time of day is it", and so forth.

PHP can also be used as a command line scripting language for shell scripts. Let's install all components that PHP has to offer on our server. In total we need four packages:

```
yum install php php-mysql php-gd php-cli
```

```
  ○ ○ ○                    CentOS 7 - LAMP Stack              ▼ ✿ | ≡ ⌐

--> Running transaction check
---> Package libzip.x86_64 0:0.10.1-8.el7 will be installed
--> Finished Dependency Resolution

Dependencies Resolved

================================================================================
 Package          Arch        Version               Repository      Size
================================================================================
Installing:
 php              x86_64      5.4.16-23.el7_0.3     updates        1.3 M
 php-cli          x86_64      5.4.16-23.el7_0.3     updates        2.7 M
 php-mysql        x86_64      5.4.16-23.el7_0.3     updates         97 k
Installing for dependencies:
 libzip           x86_64      0.10.1-8.el7          base            48 k
 php-common       x86_64      5.4.16-23.el7_0.3     updates        561 k
 php-pdo          x86_64      5.4.16-23.el7_0.3     updates         95 k

Transaction Summary
================================================================================
Install  3 Packages (+3 Dependent packages)

Total download size: 4.9 M
Installed size: 18 M
Is this ok [y/d/N]: _
```

The first package will make Apache work with PHP, the second
one is an extension through which PHP can communicate with
MariaDB and MySQL. The third package makes image resize
operations possible, and the fourth one is for writing command
line scripts (optional, but highly recommended).

There's no need to start PHP as it's not a system service, but for
the Apache integration to work we need to restart our web server:

```
systemctl restart httpd.service
```

Testing PHP

For extra credit we can test if PHP is working. Let's check the command line option first: type **php -v** to see what version of PHP we are running:

```
php -v
```

```
PHP 5.4.16 (cli) (built: Oct 31 2014 12:59:36)
Copyright (c) 1997-2013 The PHP Group
Zend Engine v2.4.0, Copyright (c) 1998-2013 Zend
Technologies
```

To test if PHP is working together with Apache, we need to get a little more involved with creating files. This will mean a slightly deeper introduction to the **vi file editor**. Feel free to skip over this step, I'll explain more about this in the next chapter.

Type the following to create a new file:

```
vi /var/www/html/test.php
```

This will bring up a rather scary blank window without any content. Don't worry though, everything is fine! Press the **a** key to enter edit mode and a cursor will appear at the top of the screen. Now type the following:

```
<?php phpinfo(); ?>
```

This is a super small PHP programme that will display the current PHP version in a web browser. **phpinfo()** is the actual function, which is ended with a semicolon, and the whole command is enclosed in opening and closing PHP tags.

A PHP capable web server (like the one we have) will see this as code that should be executed, and it will call the function - which in turn will display a lot of information about the version of PHP we have installed. Therefore this exercise is a good test to see if all is well with the whole PHP/Apache integration thing.

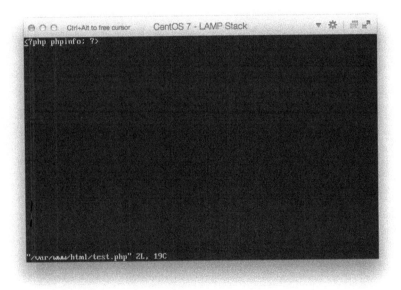

To leave this text editor, press **escape** to quit edit mode. Now press **SHIFT-Z twice** and your file will be saved. If you're back at the command line, then congratulations are in order - you've just survived your first vi experience!

Let's see if we can display our PHP programme: open your web browser and navigate to your IP address again, followed by /test.php all on one line, like this:

77

- http://12.34.56.78/test.php

If all went well you should see a very long web page similar to the one below.

This completes the installation of our LAMP Stack.

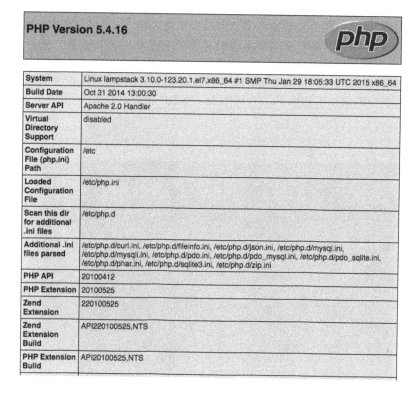

PHP Version 5.4.16	

System	Linux lampstack 3.10.0-123.20.1.el7.x86_64 #1 SMP Thu Jan 29 18:05:33 UTC 2015 x86_64
Build Date	Oct 31 2014 13:00:30
Server API	Apache 2.0 Handler
Virtual Directory Support	disabled
Configuration File (php.ini) Path	/etc
Loaded Configuration File	/etc/php.ini
Scan this dir for additional .ini files	/etc/php.d
Additional .ini files parsed	/etc/php.d/curl.ini, /etc/php.d/fileinfo.ini, /etc/php.d/json.ini, /etc/php.d/mysql.ini, /etc/php.d/mysqli.ini, /etc/php.d/pdo.ini, /etc/php.d/pdo_mysql.ini, /etc/php.d/pdo_sqlite.ini, /etc/php.d/phar.ini, /etc/php.d/sqlite3.ini, /etc/php.d/zip.ini
PHP API	20100412
PHP Extension	20100525
Zend Extension	220100525
Zend Extension Build	API220100525,NTS
PHP Extension Build	API20100525,NTS

Configuring your LAMP Stack

In this chapter we'll cover the following topics:

- securing MariaDB
- creating a user and database in MariaDB
- configuring Apache to work with rewrite rules
- accessing the LAMP Stack from a web browser

When we're finished you will be able to install web applications and access them using a web browser from other computers on your network.

Securing MariaDB

Both MariaDB and MySQL come with a script that allows us to configure the database server after the initial installation. It is very good practice to run this script before we do anything else with our database server. We only have to do this once as part of the initial configuration.

Still from the command line, we can run the script like this:

```
/usr/bin/mysql_secure_installation
```

The script will ask you a few intimidating questions, the first one of which is "what is the root user's password":

```
NOTE: RUNNING ALL PARTS OF THIS SCRIPT IS
RECOMMENDED FOR ALL MariaDB
        SERVERS IN PRODUCTION USE!  PLEASE READ
EACH STEP CAREFULLY!
In order to log into MariaDB to secure it, we'll
need the current
password for the root user.  If you've just
installed MariaDB, and
you haven't set the root password yet, the
password will be blank,
so you should just press enter here.
```

```
Enter current password for root (enter for
none):
```

It would be easy to assume that this is the same root password
we've provided during the CentOS installation - but that's not the
case. You see, CentOS and MariaDB BOTH have a system user
called root, and in both cases root is the most powerful user on the
system.

It is important to understand here that our database server is a
separate service that runs on top of CentOS, and therefore requires
an individual set of credentials.

Because we've not used MariaDB before, no root password has
been setup yet. Simply hit Enter to proceed with the script. The
next question is, "would you like to set a root password now?":

```
Setting the root password ensures that nobody
can log into the MariaDB
root user without the proper authorisation.
Change the root password? [Y/n]
```

Hit **y** and provide a password of your choice. To keep it simple
here, I suggest you use the same password as your CentOS root
password. Or, to keep it super secure, invent another strong
password and make a note of it somewhere safe. Just make sure
you understand the difference between all these passwords and
when to use them. This one will be known as your **MariaDB root
password**. Provide it a second time when prompted by the script.

The third question we must answer is "do we want to remove
anonymous users?":

```
By default, a MariaDB installation has an
anonymous user, allowing anyone
to log into MariaDB without having to have a
user account created for
them.  This is intended only for testing, and to
make the installation
```

81

go a bit smoother. You should remove them
before moving into a
production environment.
Remove anonymous users? [Y/n]

And yes indeed, we do. Hit **y** to proceed.

The fourth question is, "do we want to allow root connections
from other servers?":

Normally, root should only be allowed to connect
from 'localhost'. This
ensures that someone cannot guess at the root
password from the network.
Disallow root login remotely? [Y/n]

Let me explain why this can become important: usually only web
applications will make queries to this database server; in other
words, queries initiated on localhost. It is assumed that the
application lives on the same machine as the database server and
connects with a separate set of credentials (something other than
root).

For maintenance purposes however it can be beneficial to allow
root connections from other computers on the network too, for
example to remotely backup a database. If the server were out
there on the Internet, it means that there is a potential intrusion
point though: evildoers could try to brute-force their way in, trying
to guess the root password with several million attempts. The
script allows us to make root connections from the outside world
impossible and eliminate this potential threat.

Because our server does not live on the Internet and is only
accessible from our own network, I suggest we answer yes here
and instead block all outside connections to MariaDB later using
the firewall. Answering no will not impact our LAMP Stack's
performance though. Make any choice to proceed.

The fourth question is "should we remove a default test database?":

```
By default, MariaDB comes with a database named
'test' that anyone can
access.  This is also intended only for testing,
and should be removed
before moving into a production environment.
Remove test database and access to it? [Y/n]
```

Indeed we do, as we'll create our own databases in a moment. Answer **y** to proceed. Now for the final question: "shall we flush privileges?":

```
Reloading the privilege tables will ensure that
all changes made so far
will take effect immediately.
Reload privilege tables now? [Y/n]
```

Yes indeed, let's do that. MariaDB works with cached data in memory, and configurations and changes made manually are saved to standard files later, but not instantly. Every time a change is made we need to "flush privileges" for those changes be saved to disk and to become effective. Answer **yes** to finish the script and return to the command prompt.

```
Cleaning up...
All done!  If you've completed all of the above
steps, your MariaDB
installation should now be secure.
Thanks for using MariaDB!
```

Logging in to MariaDB / MySQL

Many MariaDB related tasks can be performed with the **mysqladmin** command from the shell. Sadly though, creating a new MariaDB user isn't one of them. We must therefore login to the database server and utilise MariaDB's own command prompt. This will present us with a new set of instructions we can use which are unrelated to the command prompt we've been using so far - even though it will look extremely similar.

I must admit that I found this terribly confusing at first. If you feel the same way, don't despair - it's a perfectly healthy reaction to have: we are humans after all, not machines. The confusion never stops, but sometimes the clear and simple explanations do. Things will become even more confusing in a moment, trust me…

Let's login to MariaDB using the following command, replacing "password" with your own:

```
mysql -u root -ppassword
```

Confusing indeed. Let me explain this from one human to another. First of all, the command to login to MariaDB is still **mysql**. That's because as we've learnt earlier, MariaDB was originally derived from MySQL and hence this login command has not been changed to maintain compatibility - much like when we used the "mysql secure installation" script in the previous chapter.

-u defines the user name we'd like to use to login to MariaDB, and -p specifies that we need a password to do so.

Note that the parameter **-ppassword** is not a typo: -p is immediately followed by your MariaDB password without a space in between. Hence, if yours would be "Mendocino", then you'd type "-pMendocino" instead of "-ppassword".

A space between -u and the user name is OK, but not between -p and the password. Go figure.

You can also leave the password blank and simply specify -p, in which case you will be prompted for your password. Either way we will end up at a new command prompt that looks a little different than the one we've been using so far:

```
Welcome to the MariaDB monitor.  Commands end
with ; or \g.
Your MariaDB connection id is 11
Server version: 5.5.41-MariaDB MariaDB Server
Copyright (c) 2000, 2014, Oracle, MariaDB
Corporation Ab and others.
Type 'help;' or '\h' for help. Type '\c' to
clear the current input statement.
MariaDB [(none)]>
```

MariaDB commands are not case sensitive, but are typically shown in all UPPER CASE to make them stand out from other (BASH) shell commands. Each command is terminated with a semicolon. I'll follow this nomenclature here to keep the confusion to a minimum.

Let's start with a quick example: list all databases that are currently on the system. Type the following:

```
SHOW DATABASES;
```

We'll see that there are three databases already on the system:

```
+--------------------+
| Database           |
+--------------------+
| information_schema |
| mysql              |
| performance_schema |
+--------------------+
4 rows in set (0.00 sec)
```

Not surprisingly, MariaDB stores its own user credentials and permissions in a database called mysql, together with information_schema. The performance_schema database is there to speed up queries.

We cannot and indeed must not use any of these databases for our own data storage.

It is common practice to create a new user and a new database for each web app we want to run. Although one user and one database can serve several applications, it's just not good practice to do work this way: applications cannot be backed up or restored on their own, and there is a potential risk one application could accidentally destroy the data of another.

Creating a Database

Let's create a new database for a web application we'll install in a moment. Since we'll install WordPress, I'll call my database wordpress. You can call it anything you like and can be more descriptive here, especially if your server will handle multiple web applications of the same kind (imagine 5 different WordPress installations - there has to be a better way than to call them wordpress1, wordpress2, and so forth).

Issue the following command, using your own devised name:

```
CREATE DATABASE wordpress;
```

MariaDB will get back to you with a status message, such as "Query OK, 1 row affected (0.01 sec)". This means everything went well.

List the databases again and see your own amongst the other three:

```
SHOW DATABASES;
+--------------------+
| Database           |
+--------------------+
| information_schema |
| mysql              |
| performance_schema |
| wordpress          |
```

```
+--------------------+
```
4 rows in set (0.00 sec)

Creating a MariaDB User

With our database in place, we'll need to create a user account that will connect to the database server and access the database. The idea here is the same as with our CentOS installation: a root user is already in place, but it shouldn't be used for everyday tasks, like communicating with our database.

Since I want to use my "wordpress" database, I'll create a user with the same name. It's common practice to create a new user for each database for security reasons. It is of course possible for one user to have access to several databases, but restricting a single user to a single database (and in turn a single application) means that one application cannot accidentally destroy data in another.

The syntax to create our user is a little complex and will make more sense in a moment:

```
CREATE USER 'wordpress'@'localhost' IDENTIFIED
BY 'password';
```

Our user name and password are given in 'single quotes'. Replace 'password' with something a tad more secure and remember it for later.

Although not strictly necessary, we can specify on which server we want to create our user. It seems silly in our situation because we only have a single server, but technically this command can perform operations on remote servers too. We only have localhost at the moment (which means "this machine"), but it's good practice to specify the host here.

With our user in place, he (or she) currently has no permissions to do anything. We need to specify what our user is allowed to do with which database. In our case, we'd like him (or her) to use our new database. We can do this with the GRANT command:

```
GRANT ALL on wordpress.* TO
'wordpress'@'localhost';
```

Here we agree to let our user 'wordpress' have all permissions on the database 'wordpress' on our local server. One peculiarity about the syntax is the way we defined our database: wordpress.* means that our user will be granted privileges on every table in the database.

We're nearly done with our MariaDB adventure, there's just one more thing to do: flush the privileges. It's a technique that the database server uses to empty all caches and write all changes to disk, which would otherwise be stored only in memory. With this statement, all our changes become final - it's good practice to call this whenever you've made a change to user privileges or databases:

```
FLUSH PRIVILEGES;
```

All that remains now is to leave the MariaDB prompt and return to CentOS. It's as easy as this:

```
QUIT;
```

MariaDB will even say "Bye" when you leave, and you're magically teleported back to the command prompt we've been using earlier.

Well done: you've survived the MySQL/MariaDB portion of configuring the LAMP Stack! In this chapter we've successfully secured the database server, created a user and a database, and granted the relevant usage rights.

Removing users and databases in MariaDB

Just in case you ever need to remove a user or a database, login as described above and use the following two commands:

```
DROP USER 'yourusername'@'localhost';
DROP DATABASE yourdatabase;
```

We have of course barely scratched the surface of what MariaDB is capable of. You can learn all about MariaDB, read the full documentation and see how it compares to MySQL at https://mariadb.org.

You'll be pleased to hear that there are GUI tools available that can help you deal with database related tasks. A popular browser based tool is **phpMyAdmin**. You can install it on your new LAMP Stack and manage users, privileges and databases from a web browser with ease. Check http://phpmyadmin.net for details.

Another tool I like to use is a Mac App called **Sequel Pro**: http://sequelpro.com - sadly it's not available for Windows. Both tools are free and open source.

Sequel Pro has several advantages: it can connect to several remote database servers, whereas phpMyAdmin is confined to localhost (as far as I know). Both apps allow you to import and export databases, but Sequel Pro can import larger databases and is not limited by the browser upload size.

Luckily dealing with databases manually is only ever necessary when we want to setup a new web application. From then on the web application will do the heavy lifting and speak to the database server on our behalf.

Another occasion for these commands is the backup and restore procedure, which we will cover later in this book.

Command Line Crash Course

Before we delve into the next section I want to give you a quick introduction on how to edit files. This is done with a command line utility called **vi**. In doing so I will also introduce you briefly to some helpful utility commands we will need for our adventure.

If you haven't used vi or any of the other commands before, you may be in for a slight shock - but you'll soon get used to how it works (as long as you put logical thinking aside). We've seen briefly how to use vi when we created the phpinfo() file. Here's the more in depth explanation I was talking about earlier.

I won't bore you with every elaborate command vi has to offer, but I will go through the following important tasks in this section:

- how to change into other directories
- how to copy files
- how to delete files
- how to open files with vi
- how to make quick changes and save them
- how to find more information about a command

That doesn't sound so hard, does it? This knowledge will come in handy on many a command line adventure going forward.

If you already know how to do this comfortably, feel free to skip this section and join me again in the next chapter on how to configure Apache.

Traversing the
directory structure

Because editing system wide configuration files is always a tad
risky - especially if you haven't done it before, and even more so
if you don't quite know what you're doing - it's always a good
idea to make a backup copy of said file before we risk screwing
something up beyond repair.

To do this without a lot of typing, we need to know how to jump
around the directory structure.

But to know where we're going, we may want to find out where
we are right now. Luckily for us there's a handy command called
pwd, which will display the current working path and show us
which directory we're currently residing in.

If you've just logged in and haven't gone anywhere, this path will
be /root. This is root's home directory. Standard users have their
home directory in /home/username.

The last portion of the path is visible as part of the command
prompt in [square brackets], along with who you are and your
server's name. The tilde symbol (~) means you're in your home
directory. In case you ever get lost, pwd will help you out and tell
you where you are.

We can change directories by using the cd command. When used without any parameters, cd will put you into your home directory, no matter how deep you've wandered into unexplored territory. Your home directory is the same directory that you've started in just after logging in via SSH. Try it now:

```
cd
```

Now change into the web root directory:

cd /var/www/html

See what happens if you issue pwd now. You could change back to your home directory by typing cd, or if you want to go "back one step", you can type

```
cd -
```

The minus operator is a bit like the back button in a web browser and will bring you back to the previous directory. Play around with cd a bit, and return back to your home directory before you try the next step.

Let's create a file now - just so that we have something to play with. It'll be empty which is just fine for our quick exercise. Let's use the touch command for that:

```
touch testfile
```

You can list all files in the current directory by using "ls" without any parameters, or "ls –la" to display more details about your files. Try it now and you should find a new testfile in that list.

Now imagine that testfile is something rather important and we want to make a copy of it. That way we can edit the original without the fear of making a mistake. To do that, we can use the cp command:

```
cp testfile backupfile
```

The first parameter here is the source file, and the second one is the destination. You'll receive no feedback unless there was an error. For example, if you try to run the command again, cp will notice that backupfile already exists and will offer to overwrite it (in which case, type y to go ahead, or n to cancel the operation).

To restore our original file, perhaps after making a fatal mistake in editing testfile, we can swap the file names around and therefore copy backupfile back to testfile:

```
cp backupfile testfile
```

Perhaps we should clean up after ourselves and not let unused files clutter up our directories. Let's assume we're done with backupfile and we no longer need it. The rm command will delete it for us:

```
rm backupfile
```

rm will ask if you would really like to remove the file - not all shell commands do this. Answer y and the file is gone.

Editing configuration files

So much for simple file operations. We will also need to edit configuration files from time to time. While this is easier from a graphical user interface, it is often quicker to do this from the command line.

The standard editor that comes with most Linux distributions is vi. It's a very old programme and can be traced all the way back to 1976. It's virtually unchanged, so we must forgive vi for being a little eccentric. You'll soon get used to editing files with it.

We can use vi simply by specifying a file name that we'd like to edit. For example, opening our testfile would simply require

```
vi testfile
```

If the file exists, it will be opened. If it does not, vi will create one for us when we save - but not when we quit the editor.

Right now there's nothing in our file, so all we see is a blank screen. vi is not in edit mode when it starts, so typing will not result in any output on the screen. Hit "a" to enter edit mode and you'll see an INSERT message at the bottom of the screen. Now you can type and move around using the standard cursor keys.

```
This is my first file in vi.
It's a little scary at first but you'll soon get used to it.

I promise...█
~
~
~
~
~
-- INSERT --
```

There are two ways to exit vi when you're done editing your file:
quit and save, or quit without saving your changes.

To quit vi, saving changes:

- press ESCAPE
- press SHIFT+Z (twice)

To quit vi without saving:

- press ESCAPE
- press the COLON key (:)
- press the Q key (q)
- press EXCLAMATION MARK (!)
- hit ENTER

This will take some practice, and I encourage you to play around
with these controls before starting to make system wide changes to
important configuration files. Create new files, add some text,
copy the file, make changes, and then quit vi with or without
saving. Do it several times until you no longer need to consult this
book. You'll soon get the hang of it, and it makes you feel like a
proper hacker!

Using man pages

vi is an indispensable tool for working on the command line and it's worth investing some time becoming confident in using it. Thankfully we won't have to write novels with it, but just in case you're curious, you can read the whole vi manual from the command line and see what else it has to offer.

If you're interested, install a package called vim (an improved version of vi that shares the same syntax), then type

```
yum install vim
```

```
man vi
```

The man command shows you additional information and an often elaborate introduction to anything you can do with a specific command. It will work with most commands on the system (except for the eccentric vi which is so minimal that it does not come with its own documentation by default - but yum install vim will make it available).

When you're in the man interface, you can

- navigate forward by pressing the SPACE bar
- go back by pressing "b"
- and quit by pressing "q"

Try to use it with the commands we've discussed in this chapter and gradually expand your command line knowledge.

Displaying file contents

There's one final thing I want to mention in regards to files: sometimes you don't want to edit a file and instead just read its contents. There are several commands that can help us do this. Two of the popular ones are cat and less. Try them both:

```
cat testfile
less testfile
```

cat will simply list all output of the file and print it to the command line, bringing us back to the command prompt to enter another command.

less on the other hand will show the file's contents page by page, much like man does. It also shares the same navigational keystrokes as man. Both have their advantages. Check the man page for both commands to find out further details.

This concludes our quick introduction to file operations on the command line. Let's start putting this knowledge to good use and configure some system wide services in the next chapter.

Configuring Apache for use with WordPress

Time to edit our first configuration file! We need to patch our web server so that WordPress and other web apps can use a feature called Permalinks. This is not mandatory but activating this feature makes reading URLs a lot easier for us humans.

Let me explain why this will come in handy.

The PHP scripts used in web apps communicate data back to the server by attaching parameters to the end of the URL. For example, to reach a specific page in WordPress, the URL would be something like http://domain.com?p=123. While this works fine for machines, the likes of you and I can't say that this is very informative.

A URL like http://domain.com/specific-page is much easier on the eye. Permalinks make this possible using something called Rewrite Rules. It's a set of rules that let Apache know that we want to turn the first URL into the second. The actual request to the application will be the same, and both URLs will work when this feature is activated. But what's displayed in the browser's URL bar, and what we share as links will look a lot nicer.

The good news is that we don't have to create these rules: WordPress (or any web app that wants to use this feature) will take care of this for us by writing to a special file called .htaccess. Apache reads this file and reacts accordingly. The .htaccess file is a plain text file. And because it starts with a dot, it will be hidden by default on Linux systems. We'll talk more about this file and what can be done with it when we install WordPress.

To enable the use of .htaccess files, we need to edit Apache's configuration file. It's located here:

- /etc/httpd/conf/httpd.conf

Because editing system wide configuration files is always a tad risky - especially if you haven't done it before - it's always a good idea to make a backup copy before we start tweaking it. Let's change into Apache's configuration directory where we'll find the above file:

```
cd /etc/httpd/conf
```

Now we'll create a backup with

```
cp httpd.conf httpd.conf.backup
```

In case something goes wrong, we'll have an untouched copy. I assume at this point that you're familiar with traversing the Linux directory on the command line, and that you know what a full file path is. If this is not something you're familiar with, I strongly advise that you check my brief introduction to editing and copying files in the earlier chapter of this book before you proceed.

Now let's edit the original file with the following command:

```
vi httpd.conf
```

This will open vi and load our Apache configuration file. When you're ready, put vi into edit mode by pressing the **a** key.

```
# This is the main Apache HTTP server configuration file.  It contains the
# configuration directives that give the server its instructions.
# See <URL:http://httpd.apache.org/docs/2.4/> for detailed information.
# In particular, see
# <URL:http://httpd.apache.org/docs/2.4/mod/directives.html>
# for a discussion of each configuration directive.
#
# Do NOT simply read the instructions in here without understanding
# what they do.  They're here only as hints or reminders.  If you are unsure
# consult the online docs. You have been warned.
#
# Configuration and logfile names: If the filenames you specify for many
# of the server's control files begin with "/" (or "drive:/" for Win32), the
# server will use that explicit path.  If the filenames do *not* begin
# with "/", the value of ServerRoot is prepended -- so 'log/access_log'
# with ServerRoot set to '/www' will be interpreted by the
# server as '/www/log/access_log', where as '/log/access_log' will be
# interpreted as '/log/access_log'.
#
# ServerRoot: The top of the directory tree under which the server's
# configuration, error, and log files are kept.
#
-- INSERT --
```

We need to find a specific portion of this file, so press the cursor down key until you find a section that begins with **<Directory "/var/www/html">** and ends with **</Directory>**. Here's the full section we need for clarification:

```
# Further relax access to the default document root:
<Directory "/var/www/html">
    #
    # Possible values for the Options directive are
"None", "All",
    # or any combination of:
    #   Indexes Includes FollowSymLinks
SymLinksifOwnerMatch ExecCGI MultiViews
    #
    # Note that "MultiViews" must be named
*explicitly* --- "Options All"
    # doesn't give it to you.
    #
    # The Options directive is both complicated and
important.  Please see
    #
http://httpd.apache.org/docs/2.4/mod/core.html#option
s
    # for more information.
```

```
    #
    Options Indexes FollowSymLinks
    #
    # AllowOverride controls what directives may be
placed in .htaccess files.
    # It can be "All", "None", or any combination of
the keywords:
    #    Options FileInfo AuthConfig Limit
    #
    AllowOverride All
    #
    # Controls who can get stuff from this server.
    #
    Require all granted
</Directory>
```

Everything that starts with a hash sign is a comment, so our <Directory> block really only contains two statements. Even though this makes the file a bit longer than it needs to be, we'll see what consequences our modifications have. Change the one line that reads **AllowOverride None** to **AllowOverride All**.

Make sure you find the right block: the AllowOverride statement appears several times in this file. We're looking for the third one.

When you're finished, press the ESCAPE key to end your editing session. Save your changes and quit vi by pressing SHIFT+Z twice and you'll find yourself back on the command line.

For the changes to take effect we need to restart Apache:

```
servicectl restart httpd.service
```

Congratulations - we're done configuring our web server!

Installing Web Applications

In this chapter we'll learn how to install a web application that can be reached from other computers on the network. This will finally put our server to good use.

Popular applications that will run on our new LAMP Stack include

- WordPress, Drupal and Joomla (content management systems)
- phpList (mailing list)
- MediaWiki (powers Wikipedia)
- phpBB (forum)

There are countless others. I will show you how to install WordPress as an example, the principle is the same for the other applications. Feel free to explore them.

I've been using WordPress since 2008 and have found many uses for it since then - including storing data on my personal server at home and collaborating with other users, either publicly on the internet, or in the privacy of my own network.

How Web Applications work in principle

The term "web application" refers to a dynamic website that is displayed in the confines of a web browser. We've been using web applications for years, much longer than the term has been in use. For example, shopping at Amazon or browsing Wikipedia means a web application is used to serve the data. We often refer to web applications as "websites" even though a lot more is going on in the back end.

Administrators will have a special area to which they can log in and perform changes or add content, without having to write code or get involved in programming. This has made the upkeep of websites a lot easier over the years. Prior to web apps, web designers and coders had to write static HTML files, and every time a change to any part of the website needed to be made, new code had to be deployed to the server.

Tasks that can be performed by a web application have become more powerful over the years; so have the web browsers we use to access them. Most current browsers will work to access web apps, both for visitors and admins alike. Perhaps the only exception is Microsoft's Internet Explorer, which still works "differently" to the rest of the crowd. Just in case things start to look "funny", consider using Safari, Firefox or Chrome.

Web applications are comprised of a series of PHP files that will be executed when the web browser makes the initial request. They do not "run continuously" like a system service on our server does. Instead they are "dead scripts" that don't really do anything until they are kicked off by the arrival of a visitor. Any type of background activity will have to be scheduled by a task, which calls a portion of the script at regular intervals.

PHP scripts in web applications are responsible for the creation of HTML content such as text data and hyperlinks, as well as images. In addition, CSS files are loaded and served to create the look and feel of the web application. CSS is used to layout font in specific sizes, determine background colour, placing images, and many other design related tasks.

The actual text data is not stored in the PHP files: instead it is served from the database server, which in turn is queried by a PHP script. For example, when the script is told to serve the front page of our web app, it could ask the database server to "show the latest 5 entries of all categories in full", or "show a list of links to all entries from January". The script then returns a combination of HTML files and CSS data to the requesting browser.

The advantage is that data can thus be served dynamically because static code is generated on the fly. As soon as a change to the content has been made by an administrator, a browser refresh will kick off the PHP script again and updates are displayed as if by magic.

To operate and install our own web apps, we as system administrators need to do the following:

- copy the web app's PHP files to the web root directory
- edit the web app's configuration file so it knows the database credentials
- trigger an initial installation script

We can do most of this from the command line as we'll see shortly. In addition, we also need a database user and a database for our web app. We've already seen how to create those in a previous chapter.

Looks like we're ready to install our first web app.

Downloading WordPress

I'm using WordPress as an example because it's extremely versatile, easy to use and install, and it has huge community support.

The latest version of WordPress can be obtained from the following link:

- http://wordpress.org/download

This web page will show a big blue download button. That's great if you have a web browser, but it's not so useful when you only have command line access like we do on our server. Thankfully the WordPress developers keep the latest version at the same location so we can use a direct link with our next shell command: **wget**.

wget is a utility that lets us download files from the internet and save them locally. Another such utility is cURL, which comes pre-installed with CentOS. wget is a bit easier to use but needs to be installed first:

```
yum install wget
```

Before we download and unpack our files, we should discuss where those files need to end up so that they can be displayed as web files.

Apache has a default directory at /var/www/html. Anything in this directory can be accessed by a web browser. This is called the web root directory, or document root directory. By default, when a browser navigates to our IP, all these files and folders are presented as a list of links, each of which would open the file when clicked. That's not much of a website though.

If we create a folder inside this web root directory, then we can directly navigate into it by appending the folder name to the IP of our server like this:

- http://12.34.56.78/subfolder

Using this principle will allow us to install as many web applications in as many directories as we like.

When a special file is present in either the web root directory or a subdirectory, the browser loads its content as HTML rather than display a list of files. Such special files start with either index, start or home and can end with .htm, .html or .php.

Usually only one of these files is present so that there's no confusion as to which ones is the default file. With PHP scripts this is commonly index.php, serving as the entry point for a web app.

Let's navigate to our web root directory so that our download can be placed directly there:

```
cd /var/www/html
```

Next, let's use wget to download the WordPress package using this simple syntax:

```
wget http://wordpress.org/latest.tar.gz
```

This will download a compressed version of WordPress into the current directory and even show us a progress bar.

The WordPress package comes in two different flavours: a .zip file and a .tar.gz file, also known as a "tarball". Those are different types of compression, but the content of the archive is the same. A tar archive is a native compression format for Linux systems and content can be extracted without the need to install another package.

To unpack our files we can use the **tar** command:

```
tar -zxvf latest.tar.gz
```

This will extract all files and folders that were contained in the archive to the current directory.

List all files using "ls" and you'll see that a new directory has been created called wordpress, which - you've guessed it - contains all files necessary to run WordPress. We no longer need the archive, so let's remove it before we forget (confirm with y):

```
rm latest.tar.gz
```

To make WordPress load from our root directory, it's helpful to copy the files from the subfolder into our current location. It's a personal preference really and it depends on how many web apps you intend to run. For this example, I will assume we're happy with a single website which lives in the document root.

To copy our files over we can use the cp command:

```
cp wordpress/* .
```

Make sure you add the dot after a space. It means "copy all files from /wordpress into the current directory".

At this point you have a choice as to how you would like other computers on the network to address your web apps: either by numeric IP (http://12.34.56.78), which will work by default and without any further system tweaks. Or, using a named URL such as http://lampstack.

It's an important decision: it's final, and it's not easily reversed.

I recommend using the named URL because it's much easier on the eye and may have benefits depending on the web app you're installing. It will require a small tweak on every computer on the network though, but it's relatively simple compared to all the other things we have done so far.

I will talk you through this in the section called "Connecting to your server from other computers".

Feel free to complete that chapter first and come back here to install WordPress. Alternatively you can follow along using a numeric IP.

Transferring File Ownership to Apache

Right now all our files in the web root directory are owned by root, and as such are only writable by the root user. But our web server Apache is in charge of maintaining the directory and it needs permission to create files and folders here during its day-to-day operations (for example, when we upload files). Hence, to avoid any nasty read/write permission problems, we need to transfer the ownership of all our web files in **/var/www/html** to Apache.

We can do this with the **chown** command:

```
chown -R apache:apache /var/www/html
```

This will do the trick, traversing into all subdirectories. On CentOS, the user of the web server process is apache, and there's also a user group called apache - hence the double barrel in the command.

We can check our success by listing all files using **ls -l** before and after the change. Here's an excerpt of our directory.

Before, all files belonged to root:

115

```
-rw-r--r--.  1 root root    418 Feb 22 05:10
index.php
-rw-r--r--.  1 root root  19930 Feb 22 05:10
license.txt
-rw-r--r--.  1 root root   7195 Feb 22 05:10
readme.html
-rw-r--r--.  1 root root   4951 Feb 22 05:10 wp-
activate.php
drwxr-xr-x.  9 root root   4096 Feb 22 05:11 wp-
admin
-rw-r--r--.  1 root root    271 Feb 22 05:10 wp-
blog-header.php
...
```

After the change they will belong to our Web Server:

```
-rw-r--r--.  1 apache apache    418 Feb 22 05:10
index.php
-rw-r--r--.  1 apache apache  19930 Feb 22 05:10
license.txt
-rw-r--r--.  1 apache apache   7195 Feb 22 05:10
readme.html
-rw-r--r--.  1 apache apache   4951 Feb 22 05:10
wp-activate.php
drwxr-xr-x.  9 apache apache   4096 Feb 22 05:11
wp-admin
-rw-r--r--.  1 apache apache    271 Feb 22 05:10
wp-blog-header.php
...
```

You must repeat this step if you install other web applications into subdirectories.

Dealing with SELinux

File permissions aside, CentOS has another level of security called SELinux. This may prevent users to create or overwrite files, even if the permissions are set correctly. SELinux can cause headaches on occasion - such as when Apache wants to create files as part of an installation. The system was developed by the NSA and as such takes security very very seriously. One small tweak aside, the system works without much intervention going forward.

I won't go into the gory details of SELinux here or explain how it works, I only want you to know that for our installation we will make it more lax than it is by default. SELinux can be run in enforcing or permissive mode, or disabled altogether (which is hardly necessary). **Enforcing** means that certain file operations will be disallowed, while **permissive** means that such operations will be logged but allowed.

To temporarily put SELinux into permissive mode, and to complete our WordPress installation without file permission trouble, we can use the **setenforce** command:

```
setenforce permissive
```

This will make SELinux allow write operations while logging unauthorised attempts. When the server is restarted, SELinux will assume its default mode of enforcing again but will not get in the way of our web application.

To learn more about SELinux and make permanent changes to its behaviour, check out this article on my website:

- http://wpguru.co.uk/2014/12/how-to-control-selinux-in-centos-7/

SELinux and Email sent from PHP Scripts

SELinux will also disallow PHP scripts to send emails so that an evildoer can't simply turn our server into a galactic spam relay station. We may need this functionality though, for example so that WordPress can send us an email to reset a forgotten password link.

Here's how to allow such emails to be sent:

```
setsebool -P httpd_can_sendmail 1
```

Note that this can take a minute or two, during which time your system appears to hang or be otherwise busy. That's normal, just be patient.

We also need to restart our web server for it to take effect:

```
systemctl restart httpd.service
```

Unlike the previous SELinux operation, this change will remain in effect when you restart your server.

Installing WordPress

Now it's time to run the WordPress installer script.

In your web browser, navigate to your server. I can reach mine using http://lampstack, but a numeric IP will work fine too. Make sure you add http:// at the front, otherwise your browser assumes you may want to search for that term instead.

You'll see the first page of the WordPress installer. Let's start by selecting a language:

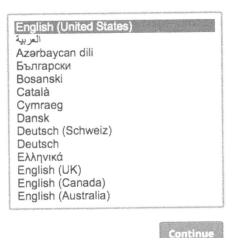

Next, the installer will ask us for some database credentials. We've set those up in an earlier chapter (I hope you've made a note of them).

The only thing we haven't addressed yet is the Table Prefix:

Each database holds tables containing data, much like an Excel spread sheet. The WordPress installer will create those tables for us so that data can be written to the database by the web application. In order for WordPress to keep track of these tables, it adds a prefix to each table. This means that several applications can share the same database, as long as the prefix for each one is different.

Should you try to run the WordPress installer a second time with the same prefix, perhaps for another website hosted in a subdirectory, it will detect that an installation is already present. In that case you can either change the prefix to something else, or create a whole new database (which I recommend).

Note that on production servers the "wp_" prefix is not recommended because it is known by potential evildoers and makes it easier to hack a WordPress installation. In our case this is not really an issue because our server is not accessible from the outside world, but in case you're planning to deploy a LAMP Stack on the internet in the future, it's something to keep in mind.

When you hit submit you'll receive a friendly message telling you that the installer can now go to work. Hit "Run the install" to proceed.

All right, sparky! You've made it through this part of the installation. WordPress can now communicate with your database. If you are ready, time now to...

Run the install

Behind the scenes, the install script will create the database schema and populate your WordPress installation with some default data. It will also create a file called wp-config.php, in which the installer will save your database credentials.

If SELinux is still enabled, or the ownership for files in the web directory are incorrect, you will receive an error here and instructions that you must create this file yourself.

Below you should enter your database connection details. If you're not sure about these, contact your host.

Database Name	**wordpress**	The name of the database you want to run WP in.
User Name	**wordpress**	Your MySQL username
Password	**password**	...and your MySQL password.
Database Host	**localhost**	You should be able to get this info from your web host, if localhost does not work.
Table Prefix	**wp_**	If you want to run multiple WordPress installations in a single database, change this.

Submit

In the next window, WordPress will ask you for a site title and user credentials, including an email address. You will use these credentials to login to WordPress and create content. Make a note of those, you will use them often.

The site title is arbitrary and can be changed easily at a later time - but your user name is final.

Welcome

Welcome to the famous five-minute WordPress installation process! Just fill in the information below and you'll be on your way to using the most extendable and powerful personal publishing platform in the world.

Information needed

Please provide the following information. Don't worry, you can always change these settings later.

Site Title

LAMP Stack

Username

versluis

Usernames can have only alphanumeric characters, spaces, underscores, hyphens, periods, and the @ symbol.

Password, twice

A password will be automatically generated for you if you leave this blank.

••••••••••••••

••••••••••••••|

Weak

Hint: The password should be at least seven characters long. To make it stronger, use upper and lower case letters, numbers, and symbols like ! " ? $ % ^ &).

Your E-mail

you@domain.com

Double-check your email address before continuing.

Privacy

☐ Allow search engines to index this site.

Install WordPress

Uncheck the Privacy tick box before we continue: when checked, every new post you create with WordPress will be submitted to several search engines. On live websites this is beneficial, but in the confines of our own network it's not necessary - as we won't get visitors other than colleagues in our office.

When you're ready, select Install WordPress. Only a few seconds later, the installer should get back to us with a SUCCESS window like this one:

Success!

WordPress has been installed. Were you expecting more steps? Sorry to disappoint.

Username	versluis
Password	*Your chosen password.*

Log In

Congratulations: you've just installed your first web app!

Introduction to Using WordPress

I do not want to make this book about WordPress, but I thought it's important to know how to log in and introduce you to the concept of the "front page" and "admin interface". Most web apps have this in common.

I'm also going to show you how to install a new theme and briefly speak about P2, a theme that can be used for easy collaboration with colleagues. It's perfect for the LAMP Stack in the office.

WordPress has two entry points, a front page and an admin area. The front page is for the benefit of visitors and can change depending on what happens in the admin area: content can be added or removed, the layout or header graphic can be changed, you name it.

To reach the front page, navigate to your server's URL. Mine is http://lampstack. You should see something like this:

Not spectacular, but infinitely changeable.

Now append /wp-admin to your URL. In my case, I'm going to navigate to http://lampstack/wp-admin. Notice that the URL will automatically change to http://lampstack/wp-login.php. The latter is the actual PHP script, and the former is a shortcut. This URL gives us access to the WordPress admin area. If we're not logged in already we're prompted for our credentials:

Username

Password

☐ Remember Me

Log In

Lost your password?

← Back to LAMP Stack

Provide them and you'll see something like this. It's called the WordPress Admin Interface:

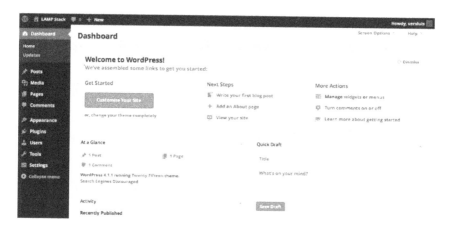

A plethora of information is available on how to get around this area, and much of it is self-explanatory. Let's create a quick post and see it come to life on the front page though, just to see how WordPress works.

Find the New button at the top of the screen, next to the plus sign. You can hover over it to bring up more options, or simply click it:

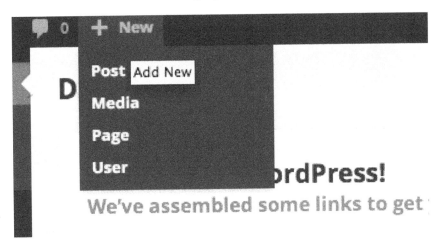

This will transport you to the New Post window. Enter a title and some text in the large box underneath. Believe it or not, this is a fully-fledged HTLM editor that can apply WYSIWYG formatting on the fly. Feel free to play with the text formatting in your own time, and if you're game, click the Add Media button to upload images and other files that can be embedded into your posts. It's powerful, enough said.

For this test, a simple title and some "lorem ipsum" style sample text will be enough to proceed. When you're done, click the blue Publish button on the right hand side. It looks like this:

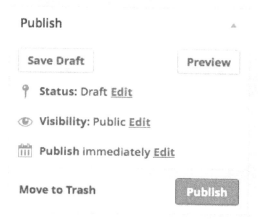

Your content is added to the database and the post will appear on the front page. More specifically, under the hood WordPress will have a discussion with the database server and add the details of your new post to the database, complete with date and revisions.

As you start writing longer posts you'll be pleased to hear that WordPress automatically saves at regular intervals - just in case the network connection to your server is interrupted, or your browser crashes. WordPress also makes use of HTML5 local storage: this feature saves your posts to the browser, just in case your network goes down at the worst moment.

To see your handy work, navigate back to the front page. You can either type your server's URL into the browser bar (in my case, http://lampstack), or you can hover over your site title in the top left corner and select Visit Site - which will do the same thing:

You should see that WordPress has managed to update the front page of your website.

Go Celebrate!

Congratulations, you've just written your very first post!

Let's not forget that you've also installed a complete operating system, configured it, added Apache, created a database, installed this Web App, and now you're using it. If that's not reason to celebrate I don't know what is 😊

131

Installing a Theme

WordPress has a concept of Themes which govern how the front page of your website looks. Changing themes means that the content of your website will stay the same but the presentation can drastically change. It's easy for web designers to create or tweak a theme using a combination of HTML, CSS, JavaScript and PHP.

Let's install a theme called P2 now to demonstrate this. From your WordPress admin interface, head over to Appearance - Themes. To reach the admin area, you can either navigate to http://lampstack/wp-admin, or if you're logged into WordPress, hover over the site title in top left corner and select Dashboard. This menu is very useful indeed - it can even transport you straight to the Themes section.

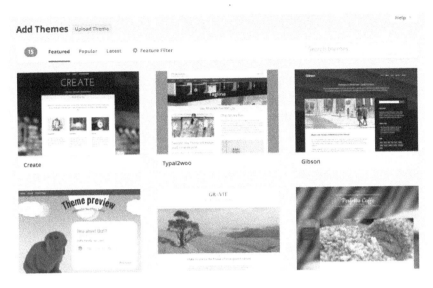

Once there you'll see a list of Themes that are currently installed in WordPress. You can switch themes simply by hovering over one of the thumbnails and then select "Activate". You can also select "Preview" to get an idea of what your website would look like without actually applying the theme.

Feel free to play with this feature, you won't break anything. To add a new theme, click the Add New option. This will let you search the WordPress repository for thousands of available free themes.

Find the search box at the top right and type P2. WordPress automatically searches in the background and will display any matches as you type - there's no need to hit return. You'll see several variations of this theme appearing. Select the first one by clicking on the thumbnail. This will open a theme preview, pulling in sample content and apply it to your selected theme. Your website hasn't changed yet, but you'll get an idea of what it would look like with the new theme in place.

You'll also see a blue Install button at the top left - click it to download the theme.

Installing Theme: P2 1.5.5

Downloading install package from https://wordpress.org/themes/download/p2.1.5.5.zip...

Unpacking the package...

Installing the theme...

Successfully installed the theme P2 1.5.5.

Live Preview | Activate | Return to Theme Installer

Click Activate to apply the theme, followed by Visit Site to see how it has changed your front page. You should now see something like this:

While this doesn't look spectacular either, notice the Facebook-esque box at the top that reads "Whatcha up to". While you can still post from the admin interface as we've discussed earlier, the P2 theme also allows you to post straight from the front page.

This functionality turns WordPress into a phenomenal note-taking and collaboration tool that can be used without the confines of the admin interface. The WordPress developers use it to coordinate a distributed team with hundreds of people around the planet.

Try it out by typing something in the box, then hit the "Post It" button. Notice how the text disappears from the box, and then magically re-appears with a subtle yellow highlight as the most recent update.

This magic is brought to you by some rather complex JavaScript code. Thankfully we don't need to understand it to enjoy it.

This new update also appears to other user who are logged in to WordPress with their own credentials, notifying everyone immediately. The same goes for comments: if another user hits the Reply link in any of the posts, they can leave a comment on a post:

Formatting for ordered and unordered lists can be applied on the fly: preface a new line with a minus sign to create a "bullet point" list; preface a new line with a # symbol to create numbered lists:

Bullet Points and Numbered Lists

- write invoice
- update system
- wash car

grind coffee
boil water
stir and enjoy

As soon as you hit Post, P2 will apply HTML tags to convert these lists:

versluis 3:10 am on February 22, 2015

Bullet Points and Numbered Lists

- write invoice
- update system
- wash car

1. grind coffee
2. boil water
3. stir and enjoy

Another fan favourite is the check box feature: preface a new line with a small letter o to generate tick boxes. These turn a post into a handy to-do list: an o will create an un-ticked check box, while a small letter x will mark it as checked.

Check Boxes

o buy milk
o schedule meeting
o phone Floyd in Cabot Cove
o write a book on how to use WordPress with P2
x this item is crossed out already

Tag it

As soon as you hit Post, P2 applies formatting and functionality to your list: logged in users can mark items simply by ticking a box, and other team members see who has marked which item:

Recent Updates

versluis 3:03 am on February 22, 2015

Check Boxes

☑ ~~buy milk~~ (@versluis)

☑ ~~schedule meeting~~ (@cavejohnson)

☐ phone Floyd in Cabot Cove

☐ write a book on how to use WordPress with P2

☑ ~~this item is crossed out already~~

P2 has so much more to offer than we can cover in this book. Because it relies on many WordPress aspects, all of those need to be fully understood to appreciate how it can help your productivity.

I encourage you to explore WordPress with P2 - it has indeed changed the way we work in the office.

I've compiled a list of all P2 features here: http://p2guide.wordpress.com.

I've also recorded a screencast on several P2 aspects too: http://wpguru.co.uk/2014/04/how-to-use-p2-screencast/

Connecting to your server from other computers

Preparing other computers to reach your LAMP Stack

Right now we can connect to our server using its numeric IP, for example ssh root@12.34.56.78 or http://12.34.56.78.

Even though this works, it's not very easy on the eye, let alone on the brain. Most humans don't like remembering strings of numbers; it's much easier for us to remember words. Thankfully there are several ways to overcome this by replacing the numeric IP with a custom domain name like http://lampstack.

I will show you two methods here: The **hosts file** method, and the **Proxy Server** method.

Let me explain what they are in the following two chapters. Before we begin, we need to know a little more about how network connections are established before we can implement these options.

When a request is made to reach domain.com, your computer needs an IP address to complete the connection. It doesn't matter if this IP is on your local network or the internet. The first point of call in this query is the **hosts file**. It's another simple text file, which has an entry for a single domain and IP address next to it.

If an IP for domain.com is found in the hosts file, that IP is used to make the connection.

If no IP is found here, then your computer queries a DNS server (it's short for Domain Name Service). Think of it as a huge database of domain names with an IP address next to them, stored in servers around the world, almost like one gigantic hosts file for the entire internet.

Which exact DNS servers are queried is part of your current machine's network setup, as part of the connection settings. It can be configured manually on every device that can connect to a network and is often setup automatically. Two popular DNS servers are those of Google and OpenDNS, but there are countless others.

The DNS server will either return an IP and a connection is made, or it may come back with "we don't know that domain", in which case the connection cannot be made and you'll receive an error message.

In our case we'd like to reach our LAMP Stack server by name too, perhaps using http://lampstack. By adding this entry and the server's IP address to our hosts file, the computer we're connecting from will reach the correct place on our network.

This is the equivalent of setting up a domain name on our own private network. You don't have to call your server "lampstack" of course; you can be as inventive as you like: give him a name, including the plus and minus signs, or even a dot at the end (as in domain.com).

One thing to keep in mind though is this: because we don't have a centralised DNS server, we have to tweak the hosts file on every computer on our network that needs to reach the server by name.

It's a simple procedure, but it's slightly different to setup depending on the platform you're using.

The hosts file

Here's what a simple hosts file looks like. This plain text file is present on Linux, macOS and Windows devices. Sometimes it contains a lot more entries depending on your operating system, but as a bare minimum most systems contain at least two lines:

```
127.0.0.1    localhost localhost.localdomain
localhost4 localhost4.localdomain4
::1          localhost localhost.localdomain
localhost6 localhost6.localdomain6
```

Both lines describe our local loopback IP (IPv4 and IPv6). This means that "localhost", "localhost.localdomain", or even "localhost4" can be used interchangeably with 127.0.0.1 on this computer. No matter which variation we choose, as long as it's on the same one line, the request will revolve to the same IP - namely 127.0.0.1.

Note that 127.0.0.1 is not your server's IP address: this loopback IP is mainly used for testing purposes. Let's not touch those two lines and leave them in one piece.

We can add our own internal domain and IP address to the bottom of this file on a new line. Follow the same pattern as above, the IP address first, followed by the name to which we want it to resolve. In my example, I'm going to add this:

```
12.34.56.78        lampstack
```

Once setup I can open my web browser and type http://lampstack which will result in my Apache Test Page. Or I can login via SSH with

```
ssh root@lampstack
```

If you want to implement the hosts file method, you should tweak every machine on the network that needs access to the server in this way, including the LAMP Stack server itself.

Let's see how to do this for every major operating system.

Editing /etc/hosts on Linux

To edit the hosts file on a Linux system, we use the vi editor again - just like we did when we edited the Apache config file. You must be root to make this change, or preface vi with sudo:

```
sudo vi /etc/hosts
```

Requests will instantly resolve to the new IP without the need to restart anything.

Editing /etc/hosts on macOS

On a Mac the hosts file is in the same location as on Linux systems (i.e. /etc/hosts). You can also edit the file with vi using the Terminal app (under Applications - Utilities, or search for it in Spotlight).

It's very unlikely that users are operating as root on a Mac (even though it can be done), let's preface our command with sudo:

```
sudo vi /etc/hosts
```

After saving the file we need to flush the hosts cache using the following command:

```
dscacheutil -flushcache
```

There won't be any feedback, but from now on your named requests will resolve to your IP.

If you find that you make changes to this file on a regular basis, or if you really dislike the command line interface, consider using a GUI tool such as **Hosts**, **Host Manager** (both on macupdate.com) or even a preference pane called **Hosts.prefpane** (on GitHub). A web search will help you find them.

Editing /etc/hosts on Windows

The hosts file also exists on Windows 7, Windows 8.1 and Windows 10. You can find it here:

- C:\Windows\System32\drivers\etc\hosts.

You must edit this file with Administrator privileges in an editor such as Notepad (Windows no longer provides a built-in command line editor).

From Windows 7 and Windows 10 you can find Notepad via **Start - All Programs - Accessories - Notepad**. Right-click it and choose **Run as Administrator**.

Now choose **File - Open** and navigate to the above location.

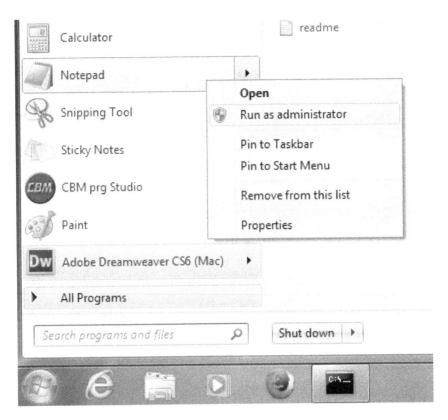

In Windows 8.1 you can find Notepad on the Metro Start Screen under **Windows Accessories**. Hold down the app icon until the bottom bar appears, the one that reads "customise". Then click on Notepad again until it's highlighted and select **Run as Administrator** in the bottom bar.

Now choose **File - Open** and navigate to the above location.

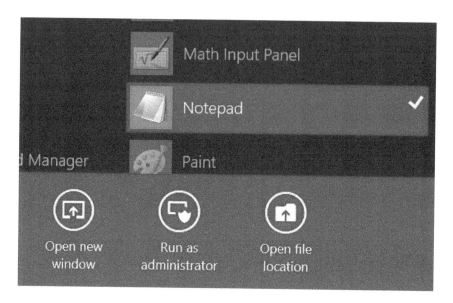

Your server name will resolve immediately without the need to restart anything.

Connecting from Mobile Devices

Even though every device has a hosts file, it is not always possible to change it. Think of mobile devices to which we have no root access.

This means we either need to forgo the benefits of named addressing, or redirect the network requests of our mobile devices through a **Proxy Server** on which we can change the hosts file.

A Proxy Server is often used as a caching server or to disguise which IP a request is coming from. For example, surfers use proxies to pretend they're visiting from a different country, or ISPs use proxies to speed up data delivery in local areas.

In simple terms, a Proxy Server is fetching data on our behalf and relays the data to us (or rather, our device). Think of a Proxy Server as a middleman in a network transaction.

To visit local websites on an iPad, or any other device that does not allow access to the hosts file, we can tweak the **Wi-Fi connection settings** to use our own server as a proxy. If we install a proxy service on it, our own server will fetch the files and relay them to our iPad, which will receive the content without querying its own hosts file.

In this chapter we'll install and configure a free Proxy Server called **Squid**. When we're finished, you'll be able to connect to websites using a domain name on your server from any mobile device.

This step is optional though: if dealing with yet another piece of the puzzle is too much for you right now, feel free to skip this chapter and return to it at a later time when the need arises.

Installing and configuring Squid

Let's enjoy some more command line adventures and login to your server as root. Squid is available via yum, and the installation is extremely simple. The following command will download and install a few related dependencies, a total of about 9MB:

```
yum install squid
```

We would also like squid to start on reboot:

```
systemctl enable squid.service
```

And finally we need to start squid with

```
systemctl start squid.service
```

That's it! You'll be pleased to hear that there is nothing else to configure. Squid should work out of the box on port **3128**, but if you ever need to tweak this or any other squid related thing, you can do so in **/etc/squid/squid.conf**.

Configuring iOS Devices

When you connect your iOS device to your local Wi-Fi network, the connection will not use a proxy server by default. You can change this under **Settings – Wi-Fi** and then tap the little info icon next to your active connection.

Needless to say, your iOS device needs to be on the same network as your LAMP Stack server.

At the bottom of this page, under "http proxy", select manual and add your server's numeric IP, and enter 3128 under Port. Leave authentication switched off.

It should look like this:

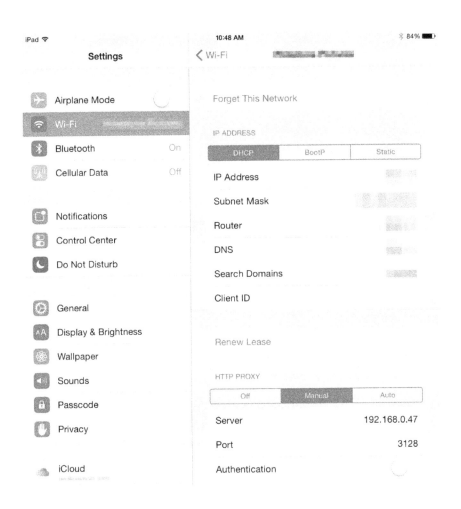

Configuring Android Devices

Android devices won't let you tweak an existing connection. To enable a Proxy Server, we need to remove the current connection and set it up again.

Head over to **Settings - Wi-Fi**, then select your active connection and remove it by tapping **Forget**.

Now pick your Wi-Fi network from the list again and check the **Advanced** tick box. Under **Proxy Settings**, choose Manual and enter your server's numeric IP address as the hostname, and enter 3128 as proxy port.

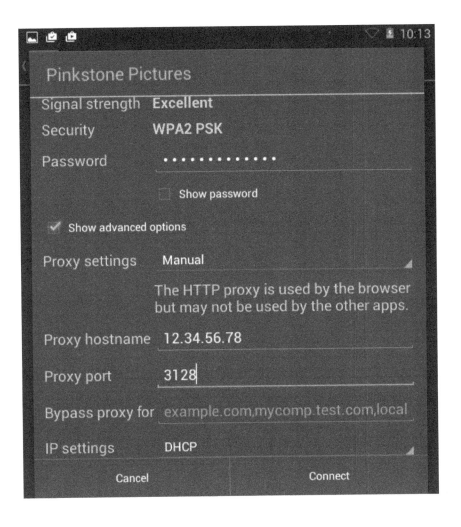

Proxy Server - Final Thoughts

With a Proxy server setup and mobile device connections tweaked, any of your named URLs will work just as they do on computers with tweaked hosts files. Try it out by navigating to your server from the web browser on your mobile device. I can reach mine using http://lampstack.

Should you not reach your web application as expected, you may experience the rather unpredictable and spurious caching technology employed by certain mobile browsers. The solution is to clear your cache, browsing history and other website data.

While we're using Squid as a Proxy Server, it will automatically cache every request you make on your mobile device as long as your Wi-Fi connection uses the proxy setting.

Depending on the speed of your server, website data from internet sources may not arrive as fast as non-cached results. In addition, Squid will leave a record of every request that has been made here:

- /var/log/squid/access.log.

To bypass the proxy and make direct requests to the Internet again, head over to your mobile device's connection and disable the proxy setting.

You can learn more about what Squid can do and how it works at the project's official website http://www.squid-cache.org

Backing up your LAMP Stack

As you add more data to your web applications, it will become a central storage hub for important information. Needless to say, should something go wrong it's vital to have a backup.

Backups mean that you can bring back your data if something happens to your server. It also makes you sleep easier at night.

There is a common misconception that the entire server needs to be backed up, perhaps using a hard disk cloning tool. While this is possible of course, it is a complex and time-consuming process and not really necessary for our server which can be rebuilt from scratch in less than an hour using our installation medium.

All we really need to keep safe is our web application data. I will demonstrate how to do this with WordPress.

We can rebuild a web app if we have a copy of

- all files in **/var/www/html**
- and a dump of all databases

In this chapter we'll learn how to do this. Because it involves multiple steps, we'll also learn how to create a simple shell script that can be run as one single command. And to finish it off, we'll setup a scheduled task so our backup happens automatically every day.

Mounting a Storage Device

Let's think about our backup strategy for a moment and start by picking a safe location: where will our backup files live?

It's not a good idea to create a backup on the internal hard drive because it is a very likely cause of failure. An external device, such as an SD card, a USB stick or external hard drive are some of the best choices.

To use any of those devices with our LAMP Stack, our storage location needs to be mounted first.

Desktop operating systems with a GUI usually mount devices automatically as soon as you plug them in. Think of those orange icons magically appearing on your Windows or Mac Desktop. Barebones Linux systems like our LAMP Stack server don't mount drives automatically, so we'll have to do a bit more hacking on the command line.

Don't worry though, it's relatively easy to do if you know how.

For this example I'm using an integrated SD card reader. I'll refer to my backup device simply as "SD card". The principle is the same for other external USB sticks and hard drives though. For simplicity's sake I won't cover how to mount network devices here.

The following command will list all attached devices on our system. Let's find out what I have on my LAMP Stack using fdisk:

```
fdisk -l
```

This will show a list of devices currently attached to our system, including internal and external drives. The fdisk command shows devices (such as /dev/sda or /dev/sdb) as well as partitions on those devices (such as /dev/sda1, /dev/sda2, and so forth).

Partitions are the formatted portions of our devices that hold the data, and they can come in several different flavours (or rather file system formats). Those formats depend on which operating system has created them:

- EXT3, EXT4, XFS (Linux)
- HFS, HFS+ (Mac)
- NTFS, FAT32, FAT (Windows)

Sadly not all operating systems can read from or write to all these formats. A Mac for example can read from a Windows NTFS partition, but it cannot write to it. Likewise, a Linux system cannot read or write HFS partitions created on a Mac. The only format ALL current operating systems can read from and write to is Microsoft's FAT32.

It's lacking several high-performance features such as journaling, and it's limited to a maximum file size of 4GB, and a single partition is limited to a size of 2TB. Keeping these things in mind, our web application will unlikely create anything bigger than 4GB, and the benefit of being able to read our SD card on other machines greatly outweighs the drawbacks.

It is of course possible to add packages to CentOS that allow read/write access for other formats, so rest assured though that if you absolutely must change the partition flavour from FAT32 to something else, you can explore this at your own leisure.

Before we can use our SD card it needs to be formatted. I strongly recommend to do this in either Windows or Mac because it's much easier than to do this from the command line in Linux. I will explain how to do this in the Extras chapter of this book because there are several intimidating steps to the whole process. For now I'm assuming you've formatted your SD card already.

Here's the output I get on my system from the fdisk -l command. It lists the following very long and slightly scary list:

```
Disk /dev/sda: 68.7 GB, 68719476736 bytes, 134217728
sectors
Units = sectors of 1 * 512 = 512 bytes
Sector size (logical/physical): 512 bytes / 4096
bytes
I/O size (minimum/optimal): 4096 bytes / 4096 bytes
Disk label type: dos
Disk identifier: 0x000980ba
   Device Boot      Start         End       Blocks
Id   System
/dev/sda1    *       2048     1026047      512000
83   Linux
/dev/sda2         1026048   134217727    66595840
8e   Linux LVM
Disk /dev/mapper/centos-swap: 2181 MB, 2181038080
bytes, 4259840 sectors
Units = sectors of 1 * 512 = 512 bytes
Sector size (logical/physical): 512 bytes / 4096
bytes
I/O size (minimum/optimal): 4096 bytes / 4096 bytes
Disk /dev/mapper/centos-root: 44.4 GB, 44354764800
bytes, 86630400 sectors
Units = sectors of 1 * 512 = 512 bytes
Sector size (logical/physical): 512 bytes / 4096
bytes
I/O size (minimum/optimal): 4096 bytes / 4096 bytes
Disk /dev/mapper/centos-home: 21.7 GB, 21655191552
bytes, 42295296 sectors
Units = sectors of 1 * 512 = 512 bytes
```

```
Sector size (logical/physical): 512 bytes / 4096
bytes
I/O size (minimum/optimal): 4096 bytes / 4096 bytes
Disk /dev/sdb: 7950 MB, 7950303232 bytes
255 heads, 63 sectors/track, 966 cylinders
Units = cylinders of 16065 * 512 = 8225280 bytes
Sector size (logical/physical): 512 bytes / 512 bytes
I/O size (minimum/optimal): 512 bytes / 512 bytes
Disk identifier: 0x00000000
   Device Boot      Start         End       Blocks
Id  System
/dev/sdb1                 1         967     7759872
b   W95 FAT32
Partition 1 has different physical/logical beginnings
(non-Linux?):
     phys=(1023, 254, 63) logical=(0, 130, 3)
Partition 1 has different physical/logical endings:
     phys=(1023, 254, 63) logical=(966, 145, 11)
```

It's easy to panic when you see such a list at first glance. All I have on this system is an internal hard drive and my SD card, so there's a lot of additional information here. Let's decipher what it all means.

A line starting with Device will show us how many partitions are on which device and what they are called. For example, my internal hard disk is known as /dev/sda and it contains two partitions known as /dev/sda1 and /dev/sda2. Just above this line I can see a block that tells me the total size of the drive (68.7GB) and what this device is called: /dev/sda.

Further down the list I can see another line starting with Device, and above it another block stating that /dev/sdb is 7950MB, with one partition called /dev/sdb1. That's my SD card! Not big enough to hold large backups, but certainly good enough for my text based office data and a few images. It's probably also really slow to access - but that's all fine for our purposes.

For CentOS to be able to talk to the device we need to create a mount point. We do this by creating a standard directory first, and then we will mount the device to it. When we henceforth refer to the directory, we will in fact be reading from or writing to our device. Let's create a directory using the mkdir command first:

```
mkdir /backup
```

Now we'll use the **mount** command to make the first partition on our SD card accessible in this directory:

```
mount /dev/sdb1 /backup
```

Since there's nothing on the card yet, ls -l won't give us any output - but we could check how much free space we have using the df command:

```
df -h /backup
```

```
Filesystem      Size  Used Avail Use% Mounted on
/dev/sdb1       7.4G  3.2G  4.3G  42% /backup
```

The -h parameter shows data in a more human-friendly format rather than plain bytes, it's much easier on the eye. Looks like there is something on my SD card after all.

If you ever want to remove the drive while your server is running, make sure to unmount the card first. It's the same as "safely ejecting" your devices from desktop computers. Here's why this is important: some data may have been cached to memory to make read/write operations appear much faster than they actually are. When we tell the system that we'd like to unmount the device, the operating system writes all cached data from memory to the disk.

The unmount command knows what to do if you either specify the directory or the physical device in question. Both these commands will do the same:

```
umount /backup
```

```
umount /dev/sdb1
```

Make sure your SD card is mounted before continuing with the
next chapter, where we discuss how to create our first backup.

Creating backups of our Web Applications

Backups are most effective when they are as simple as possible. It's very easy to overcomplicate a strategy for backups by trying to be too clever.

In our case we want to take a snapshot of all current web applications installed in /var/www/html and export all databases. In the event of a hard drive crash we can quickly build a new server, then copy all content from our SD card back to /var/www/html and import all databases. This should get us up and running again.

Once the backup has been written, you could go ahead and create a ZIP archive of the whole content every day for rolling backups. Or, instead of copying the data to an SD card, you may want to copy it to a different geographical location in case the house burns down.

For our server project we will keep it simple and copy all files to the SD card we've mounted earlier.

I will first introduce you to the commands necessary to create a backup. Then will show you how to write a shell script so we can run a sequence of commands. And to finish this chapter, I will show you how to execute a backup script automatically so we don't have to think about creating backups manually.

Backing up a Database

Let's begin by reading out our databases to a flat file. We shall do this in the same web root directory that all our other application files live in, perhaps in a designated folder.

Let's create one using **mkdir**:

```
mkdir /var/www/html/databases
```

We can use the **mysqldump** command to export a database to a file, using MariaDB credentials and the database in question. Here's how to export our wordpress database from earlier:

```
mysqldump -u root -ppassword wordpress >
wordpress.sql
```

Remember the -ppassword syntax? The parameter -p is followed without a space by your password. By using the root user here we can access any database on the server without having to worry about access privileges.

The "greater than" sign diverts any output from this command to a file, without which we would simply see a lot of text displayed on screen. This text describes every detail of our database. By diverting the output to a file (called wordpress.sql), we can capture the text and use it to rebuild the database later.

If you have more than one database, repeat this command to create separate files. To make sure the file is saved in our desired location, prefix it with the full path. In our case that's

- /var/www/html/databases/

While the above approach will create a valid backup of the actual database, it does not backup the user we have created for the database (which was also called wordpress). That's because MariaDB and MySQL save user credentials in the **mysql** database, and to save our users we would have to backup that database too.

Thankfully there is an option read out all databases at once - including the mysql database - with the following command:

```
mysqldump -u root -ppassword -- all-databases > everything.sql
```

I'm mentioning both options here because using the latter one has implications when it comes to restoring your databases:

If you have a single file for all databases, then your only option is to restore the entire database server. This procedure will overwrite everything else, including any existing data you may want to keep. Imagine you had an existing database server that already hosts several working web applications, and you would like to add a backup from the current server, there is no easy way to separate a single database out.

However, to simply rebuild the entire database server, the "all-databases" option is just perfect.

Because the operation doesn't take long, I recommend to double up and backup single databases as well as "all-databases" so that any potential restore scenario can be completed without headaches.

I will talk in greater detail about how to restore a backup in another chapter of this book.

Next, let's backup the files.

Copying files

We've already seen how to copy files using the cp command. We could utilise this command to copy data from /var/www/html directory to /backup like so:

```
cp -r /var/www/html /backup
```

The trouble with this approach is that cp will stop and ask if we're happy to overwrite every existing file. We could simply prepend it with y | (pipe) and change the command into the following:

```
y | cp -r /var/www/html /backup
```

This will answer YES every time cp has a question, but it's a clunky approach. In addition, with large amounts of data to be copied, it would be a waste of time and bandwidth to copy every file even if it hasn't changed. Let's face it: many files will stay the same over time. Think of large video files and images that would take several minutes to copy.

Likewise, files that have been deleted deliberately - perhaps to clear out some space - would not automatically be deleted from the backup. This would mean that our backup would become much larger than our original installation needs to be as time goes by.

To avoid all those problems we can use an extremely clever command called **rsync**. As the name suggests, it keeps two directories in perfect sync. It's not installed in CentOS by default, so let's bring it in with our old friend yum:

```
yum install rsync
```

rsync is a powerful tool with a vast array of options, even though it also has a few weird habits. As long as we know about those and treat it right, rsync can become another friend in our adventures on the command line. The basic syntax is this:

```
rsync -r source/ destination
```

The -r option means "copy things recursively", meaning it will include content in all folders and sub folders.

But rsync doesn't simply copy files from one directory to another: instead it checks to see if a source file already exists on the destination and if it's up-to-date. If that's the case, the file is skipped and only new files are copied. This allows two directories to be kept in sync without unnecessary file operations.

Another benefit of rsync is that our destination does not have to be a local target: rsync is happy to sync directories between different servers. We simply have to preface the destination with credentials and an IP or URL like so:

```
rsync -r source/ user@12.34.56.78:/destination
```

Sadly we cannot provide a password with this command, so it will always stop and ask for user input. This makes it difficult to use in automated scripts.

rsync has an option that lets us transfer only the changed portions of a file: imagine a text file that had a chapter added in the middle of the document. When we use this option, rsync's clever compression algorithm can see that most of the file is unchanged, only transfers the changed portion of the file and brings the destination up to date. It's as if it had copied the entire file at a fraction of the time.

The option is used by default when the source and destination are not on the same server, but it has speed benefits even when used locally. To engage this option we can pass the --no-W parameter (it stands for "don't copy entire files"):

```
rsync -r --no-W source/ destination
```

And finally, if we want files to be deleted on the destination if they have been deleted on the source, we can pass --delete:

```
rsync -r --delete source/ destination
```

There are many more parameters we can pass, but the above should be plenty to get us started. Remember you can always check man rsync for more details.

Let's copy our files from the web root directory to the SD card now using rsync. Here's what the whole command looks like, including full paths for our server:

```
rsync -rvz --delete --no-W /var/www/html/
/backup
```

That's a LOT of options. In detail, we ask rsync to sync all files and subfolders in /var/www/html to /backup, deleting files that may not be in the source folder anymore.

Furthermore, we would like to use that magic "partial file" algorithm to save bandwidth and time during the operation. The -z option applies compression during the transfer, and the -v option will provide some verbal feedback while we run the command. The first time we execute this it will take a little longer than on subsequent runs.

Creating a shell script for our backup

Now that we know how to export the database and copy files, we would have to execute two rather complex commands every time we want to run a backup. Chances are that in a week we'll have forgotten how to do it.

The good news is that computers are fantastic at remembering such complicated instructions! Let's put this aspect to good use now with the help of a **shell script**.

A shell script is a simple text file in which we can tie a series of commands together. As soon as we run the script, all commands are executed in sequence, just as if we had typed them in one after the other. It's really simple, and it works with every shell command we've seen so far.

There are two small things we need to know about writing shell scripts though:

- a script we want to execute needs to have the right **file permissions**
- the first line of a script needs to start with **#!/bin/bash** to work

If a file does not have the "execution bit" set, Linux will refuse to run it for security reasons. Turning any file into an executable file in Linux is easy using the **chmod** command:

```
chmod +x yourfile
```

Thankfully amending the file permissions only has to be done once, it will remain intact after subsequent edits. Once set, we can run our shell script like this:

```
./yourfile
```

The dot slash at the beginning is necessary to ask the shell to look in the current directory. If we leave out the dot slash, the command line will get back to us with a "command not found" error because it didn't know where to find it.

Let's write a quick shell script and try it: we will use vi again which will automatically create a file for us if one by that name does not already exist:

```
vi hello
```

Remember how vi works? Press the **a** key to enter edit mode, then type or paste the following two lines. When you're finished, press **ESCAPE** to relinquish edit mode, followed by **SHIFT+Z** (twice) to save your file:

```
#!/bin/bash
echo "Hello!"
```

Now we need to give our file the correct permissions:

```
chmod +x hello
```

And run the script:

```
./hello
```

Congratulations, you've written a shell script! Here's what happened:

The mysterious first line starts with what's known as a "she-bang", and it lets the shell know where to find an interpreter for the script that follows. Our shell script uses BASH, because that's what our command line uses, but you could also specify the path to another scripting language such as PHP or Python, and adjust your script accordingly.

The echo command simply writes what follows, in our case "Hello!". You can add as many commands here as you like, adding one command per new line.

Commonly shell scripts end with **.sh** so that we get an idea what a file does when we list a directory, but as seen above this is not strictly necessary. Shell scripts can also contain comments that are not executed. They allow us to describe what an action does so we remember later on.

To add a comment, start a new line with the # (hash symbol) and type any text you like.

Let's create a simple backup script now, including comments. We'll start by creating a new file using vi again. I'll call mine backup.sh:

```
vi backup.sh
```

You know the drill with vi, so here's the code for the script:

```
#!/bin/bash
#
# Super Simple Backup Script
# ==========================
# v1.0
# Date: (today)
# Author: (you)
# delete previous database file
```

174

```
rm /var/www/html/databases/wp.sql
# create new database backup
mysqldump -u root -ppassword wordpress >
/var/www/html/databases/wp.sql
# sync all files
rsync -rz --delete --no-W /var/www/html/ /backup
# also sync the .htaccess file
rsync -rz --delete --no-W
/var/www/html/.htaccess /backup
```

The comments make this script self-explanatory. Feel free to increase the version number as you apply changes to the file, for example adding further databases, or adding echo statements so the script outputs text as it works.

Note that I have removed the -v option from the two rsync lines, which means the sync procedure will be run silently. Feel free to add it back if you wish.

One intricacy of the rsync command is that it does not copy hidden files in the main directory - even though it does do so in sub folders. It's a feature rather than a bug (or so I was lead to believe). Only one file in our WordPress installation is affected, so I'm simply adding a second rsync statement to copy the all important .htaccess file over as well.

Let's give our script execute permissions:

```
chmod +x backup.sh
```

Voila - now we can run it using

```
./backup.sh
```

A lot can be done with shell scripts, and this was a mere barebones example. A nice addition would be if the script would send us an email every time it runs and perhaps generate a log that we can check for potential problems, or just to verify that everything went well. This can be useful when the script runs unattended - as we'll discuss in the next section.

It's also feasible to have updates applied to the sever while we're running something on a regular basis, simply by adding **yum -y update** to the end of the script. I encourage you to be creative and explore such features in your own time, and amend the above or even create your own personalised backup script as you see fit.

I have created a more elaborate version of the above script on GitHub:

- https://github.com/versluis/LAMP-Stack-for-Humans

You're welcome to take look at it and use it as a starting point, or edit it if you like. I've added several options such as email notifications and log output.

Automatically executing your backup script

It would be cumbersome and error prone if we had to login to our server once a day and run the backup script manually. I can only speak for myself here, but I regularly forget things at the supermarket, which means that it's likely that I'll forget to execute manual backups just as regularly.

Computers on the other hand are great at remembering mundane tasks, as long as they are always on - which should be the case with our server.

This is an important point to remember: scheduling your backup for 3am in the morning is no good if your server will be off at that time. Like most computers in data centres, I'm assuming that your server will be left on and ready for requests 24/7.

CentOS has a built-in service called **cron**. It's enabled by default and runs system wide tasks on a regular basis, such as rotating log files and many other things that need to be done (most of which we usually never think about).

We can hook into this cron mechanism in two ways: we can either schedule things at specific recurring intervals using the **crontab** command. An instruction would be something like "run this every Wednesday at 11:26am".

Or, if we are less concerned about the exact time, we can simply copy our script to a certain location at which it will be called automatically at regular intervals.

I will show you both approaches here, and will leave the final decision up to you.

Let's start with the simpler one first: copying your script to a **cron folder** for regular automatic execution. Run the following command to see the location of several folders:

```
ls /etc/cron*
...
/etc/cron.daily:
0yum-daily.cron   logrotate   man-db.cron
/etc/cron.hourly:
0anacron   0yum-hourly.cron
/etc/cron.monthly:
/etc/cron.weekly:
```

The asterisk will show us all entries beginning with cron. Notice that last four folders in the list:

- /etc/cron.daily
- /etc/cron.hourly
- /etc/cron.monthly
- /etc/cron.weekly

Scripts in those folders are automatically executed as described by the folder. We can also see that some scripts are already present in those folders, such as logrotate in the daily folder.

To add our own script to the daily schedule, we can simply copy it to the /etc/cron.daily folder:

```
cp backup.sh /etc/cron.daily
```

Simple and effective, and probably good enough for most casual user's needs. If you're curious (like me) and you want to know when exactly the scripts in these folders are executed, I can tell you that

- hourly tasks happen at 1 minute past the full hour
- daily tasks happen at 04:02 (am) in the morning
- weekly tasks happen at 04:22 (am) in the morning every Sunday
- monthly tasks happen at 04:42 (am) in the morning on the first of every month

Calling scripts at specific times

If you need to run a script at precisely 11:43am every Monday rather than "sometime this week", then you can use the **crontab -e** command. This is the more difficult of the two approaches I mentioned earlier.

If you're content with the earlier approach, feel free to skip this section.

When you call crontab -e, the command will open a vi session for a text file, which can contain as many scheduled tasks for the current system user as you like, one per new line. Since we're logged in as root, root will execute any script referenced in this file.

The syntax is a tad confusing, so let me give you an example for the scenario above:

```
43 11 * * 1 /full/path/to/script.sh
```

At the beginning of each line you'll see five positions, separated by a space. Counting from the left:

- minute (0 to 59)
- hour (0 to 23, as in military time)

- day (1 to 31, the day must of course exist for this to work)
- month (1 to 12, as in January to December)
- day of the week (0 to 7, either of which is Sunday, 1 is Monday, etc)

Following these six numbers is the full path to the command we want to execute. Now our example line makes a bit more sense: it calls the sample script at 11:43 every Monday.

Instead of single numbers we can also specify ranges, such as 1-5 (as in Monday to Friday, or the first to the fifth of every month). In addition we can specify something like "every third day" by using the asterisk and a slash, as in */3.

Some scripts may generate output that would be sent as an email to root@localhost – probably not an email address we would ever check. To specify a different email address, you can add the following line to the top of the file:

```
MAILTO="you@yourdomain.com"
43 11 * * * 1 /full/path/to/script.sh
```

If you would rather not see any output that is generated from a script, we can discard any text by diverting it to **/dev/null**, much like we would divert output to a text file using the "greater than" sign:

```
MAILTO="you@yourdomain.com"
43 11 * * * 1 /yourscript.sh > /dev/null 2>&1
```

/dev/null is a "virtual device" for the purpose of throwing things away without generating an error message. The weird number combination following it (2>&1) makes sure that both regular text output as well as error messages are diverted.

Adding scheduled tasks in this manner takes a bit of practice, but it allows for full flexibility in your backup schedule. Remember to add the execute permissions to a file you would like to call using a scheduled task, otherwise it won't be executed!

181

If your server is on all the time, I strongly recommend the easier approach from earlier - just make sure you copy the script over to the relevant folder every time you make a change.

For more information about editing the crontab file, please refer to the CentOS documentation about this topic:

- https://www.centos.org/docs/5/html/Deployment_Guide-en-US/ch-autotasks.html

Restoring your backups

A rather important point of any backup strategy is often overlooked: how do we **restore** the backup we've just created? Hopefully this isn't something we need to do on a regular basis. But when the time comes, it's good to have it written down somewhere.

In essence, we'll follow the steps for creating a backup in reverse order. I'm assuming here that you have an empty database server and a completely empty web root directory, much as if you had just rebuilt the server.

If that's the case, proceed with the next step.

Practicing a restore

If you would like to practice restoring a backup, you can **delete all content from the web directory** using the following command:

```
rm -rf /var/www/html/*
```

There is no going back from this, and you will not be asked if you'd like to go ahead. **Use this command with extreme caution!**

There is no such easy command for MariaDB, so you'll have to drop each database manually with

```
mysqladmin -u root -ppassword drop name-of-
database
```

You will be prompted if you would really like to go ahead. Repeat this step for every database you'd like to remove.

In addition, you may want to remove any MariaDB users that have been created. You should do this by logging into MariaDB as root, and then execute the "drop user xyz" command as discussed in a previous chapter.

Restoring your files

Assuming you have already mounted your SD card or other backup device to the /backup directory as described earlier, we can copy all files back using the **cp** command:

```
cp -r /backup/* /var/www/html/
```

When the command has finished, we must once again fix the file ownership as these won't be preserved on the SD card (mainly because Apache, the original owner, does not have write permissions to that card by default).

Read/write/execute permissions will stay intact though. The following command will take care of giving the ownership back to Apache:

```
chown -R apache:apache /var/www/html/*
```

Restoring your databases

Restoring a single database is done with the **mysql** command. This time we're using the "smaller than" sign to read data from a file back into MariaDB (or MySQL).

If you have created a backup with the **--all-databases** option you can go ahead and replace every user and every database on the system like this:

```
mysql -u root -ppassword < all-databases.sql
```

Note that this will **overwrite everything that's currently stored in MariaDB**, including user accounts and existing databases. This is a good approach if you'd like to replace one server with another, but not if you're migrating data into an existing working system.

If you have instead backed up databases individually, then we have a little more work to do. First we need to create an empty database again so we can populate it with the data in the file. Let's say our database was called "wordpress", we can create an empty database by that name with

```
mysqladmin u root -ppassword create wordpress
```

Now we can use the **mysql** command to bring our data back:

```
mysql -u root -ppassword wordpress <
/var/www/html/databases/wordpress.sql
```

Right now we haven't got a user who could let our web app use that database, so we need to create one manually again and grant him/her permissions to use this database. I've described this step in in an earlier chapter.

Sadly this is not possible using the mysqladmin command, so we need to login to the MariaDB command prompt. Here's a quick refresher:

```
mysql -u root -ppassword
```

Now create a new user ("wordpress" in our case):

```
CREATE USER wordpress IDENTIFIED BY 'password';
```

and grant the relevant permissions:

```
GRANT ALL ON wordpress.* TO wordpress IDENTIFIED
BY 'password';
```

Before we leave:

```
FLUSH PRIVILEGES;
```

Type exit to quit the MariaDB session.

————————————-

At first it seems that the **--all-databases** option is the more convenient of the two methods. That's definitely correct if there is nothing on the new server you want to keep.

However, if you would like to add a web application to a working system that already has data, you must use the second approach.

I thought it's worth showing you both just in case.

Enabling the Firewall

Remember that we disabled the firewall earlier? Time to bring it back and learn more about it. Firewalls are useful when the server is up and running, but they can get in the way of things when you're configuring the server during its initial setup.

To see if the firewall is currently active, let's check its status. On CentOS 7 the daemon running the firewall is called **firewalld** and we can check it like this:

```
systemctl status firewalld.service

firewalld.service - firewalld - dynamic firewall
daemon
   Loaded: loaded
(/usr/lib/systemd/system/firewalld.service;
disabled)
   Active: inactive (dead)
```

The last line at the bottom tells us it's currently not active.

On CentOS 6 the firewall service is called **iptables** and we can check it like this:

```
service iptables status
```

If inactive, you'll get a simple one-liner stating that "Firewall isn't running". If the service is active you'll get a long list of rules that are being applied.

To activate the firewall, use the same command as above, replacing status with start (or restart of you'd like to stop and start it again):

```
// on CentOS 7
systemctl start firewalld.service

// on CentOS 6
service iptables start
```

You won't see any output from this command unless there was a problem.

Nothing appears to have happened here - however if you try to visit that web application we've setup earlier, you'll see that the browser has a problem loading your URL (like http://lampstack). Totally not what we want - yet a great demonstration that our firewall is hard at work.

The browser can't open the website because requests to our IP on all ports except for 22 (the SSH session) are blocked. Switching the firewall off again means all requests get through, and the website is displayed just as before.

We can apply specific rules to the firewall and let requests on certain ports get though, for example web server requests on port 80, while leaving all others ports closed. Or we could restrict SSH logins to our own IP address, so that way evildoers cannot break into our server by attempting to guess our password several million times, a practice known as brute-force attack.

The firewall allows us to open only a select few entry points to the server while leaving many others closed off and therefore secured. This is less important on our office server and more relevant on live servers out there on the internet, but it's good to understand the concept.

You may have seen scary rules such as this one, opening firewall ports manually from the command line:

```
firewall-cmd --zone=public --add-port=8443/tcp -
-permanent
firewall-cmd --zone=public --add-port=8447/tcp -
-permanent
firewall-cmd --reload
```

These are different for CentOS 7 and CentOS 6, and while a little easier to grasp for CentOS 7, they are really not very user friendly to apply and tweak.

Thankfully there's a tool that will allow us to manage our firewall rules with a simple and convenient interface. It's much easier to use and works the same on CentOS 6 and CentOS 7, applying those scary rules under the hood on our behalf. It's called **system-config-firewall.**

Let's install it using yum:

```
yum install system-config-firewall-tui
```

We can start the tool without any commands by using

```
system-config-firewall-tui
```

Our firewall needs to be disabled before we can start the tool, and you will receive a warning message should the firewall be active. To disable it, use this on CentOS 7:

```
systemctl stop firewalld.service
```

and likewise, to disable the firewall on CentOS 6, use this:

```
service iptables stop
```

Then start the tool again. You'll be greeted with a friendly Firewall Configuration screen such as this one:

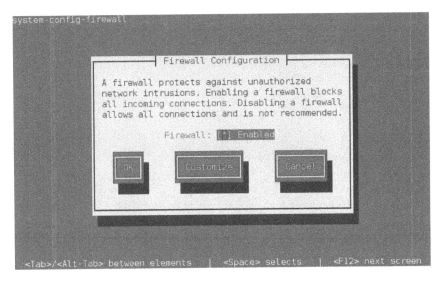

This type of presenting an interface is called a TUI or "text-based user interface". They can be very handy - if you know how to navigate the interface.

Here's how to do that:

- use the cursor keys to move up and down
- use the SPACE bar to select items
- use TAB to choose the next option
- and once selected, hit RETURN

Let's go through the options of our command line tool:

Make sure the "Enabled" option is enabled so that the firewall will be switched on as soon as we leave the tool, then select "Customize" to continue to a selection screen.

system-config-firewall has several built-in pre-sets, such as DNS, FTP, Mail, standard and secure http ports and many others. To allow connections to our website, we need to enable the following:

- SSH

- Secure WWW (HTTPS)
- WWW (HTTPS)

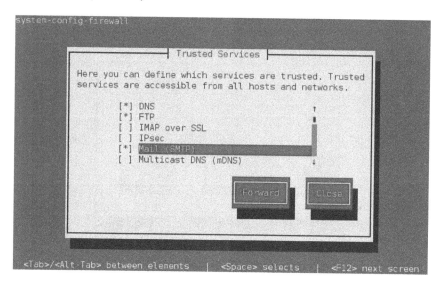

If you need to open any further ports, feel free to come back here anytime as you start using your server for other tasks (for example, file sharing via FTP).

Select Forward to continue.

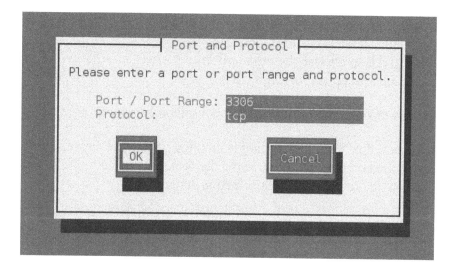

If you need to open other specific ports, you can do so on the "Other Ports" screen: define both the port and the protocol, and your desired port will be opened.

In the above screenshot I'm opening port 3306 for incoming MySQL traffic, which will allow me to remotely connect to the MariaDB server and manage databases in case the need should arise.

Select OK when you're done, followed by "Close" to return to the main screen. When you're ready, select OK and your new firewall rules are applied. You'll see yet another screen mentioning IPv6 - don't worry about it and select OK again. This should return you back to the command line.

Now open your web browser and try to navigate to your web application again. This time it should load fine, just as it did when the firewall was switched off. You may want to verify that the firewall is definitely running - and I trust you know how to do this by now.

Before we leave this chapter, there's just one more thing to do: let's make sure that our firewall is started when our server reboots. To enable this feature in CentOS 7, use this:

```
systemctl enable firewalld.service
```

On CentOS 6 you can achieve the same with this:

```
chkconfig iptables on
```

Congratulations, you've just configured the server's firewall and applied some rather difficult rules!

That's all, folks!

We're nearly at the end of our journey, and all other topics in this book are optional. I've included them for future reference, and to add detail that would have otherwise interrupted and overwhelmed the flow of the previous topics.

If you made it to this part of the book, WELL DONE FOR HANGING IN THERE!

By now you should be up and running with your server as well as your favourite web application.

I know this wasn't easy, and I've had my share of headaches and frustrations over the years. Remember that "practice makes perfect", and don't be afraid to tear down your server and start again from scratch – especially if something isn't quite working as it should.

GitHub Repository

I have added the backup script and other related code snippets for this book on GitHub:

- https://github.com/versluis/LAMP-Stack-for-Humans

Should you need any help in following the instructions in this book, or if something isn't working as you expect it, share your thoughts as an "Issue" at the above address.

And finally, if you liked (or disliked) this book, please leave a quick review and let other readers and myself know your thoughts.

Have fun, and Happy Hacking!

JAY VERSLUIS

Installing CentOS 6 (32 bit)

If your hardware does not support 64-bit, or if you would like to run CentOS 6 for other reasons, then this part of the book is for you.

I have dedicated a whole chapter to CentOS 6 because it's still a strong operating system, and installing it on our local server is very different from installing CentOS 7.

One major difference is that it's tough to connect CentOS 6 to a Wi-Fi network with the minimal installation option. This is no problem if you're using a wired connection, but many have tried and failed to connect to their Wi-Fi network without the help of GNOME. We'll discuss how to do this and make sure the system boots up so that wireless connections are possible.

Another difference between CentOS 6 and CentOS 7 is how we need to start system services.

In this chapter I will discuss such details, and by the end we will have the 32-bit version of CentOS 6 installed on your server.

This chapter is not mandatory reading if you're happy with CentOS 7.

Choosing a CentOS 6 disk image

Just as with CentOS 7, you have a choice between downloading the minimal CentOS 6 image, or the Full DVD 1 ISO. Please refer to the instructions in the previous chapter on how to transfer the image to DVD media or a USB stick.

Technically we will only need the minimal image - IF we wanted to connect our server using an Ethernet cable. The CentOS 6 installer is aware of wired connections and can set these up without problems.

However, if you intend to run your server on a wireless (Wi-Fi/WLAN) connection, you must choose the **Full DVD 1 ISO image**. The reason for this is that we need to install a full Desktop environment that we will utilise to create the Wi-Fi connection. And we need that Internet connection to install additional packages for our LAMP Stack.

Even if you intend to connect your server via Wi-Fi at a later stage, I strongly recommend using the Full DVD 1 ISO image. The following instructions will assume that we want to setup a wireless connection.

When you're ready, boot your server from the DVD or USB stick and moments later you should see the CentOS 6 installer going to work.

Using the CentOS 6 Installer

Choose the first option that reads "Install or upgrade an existing system".

If you run into trouble with your hardware and you do not see a picture going forward, feel free to choose the second option which will launch the installer using a basic video driver.

Hit Enter to continue.

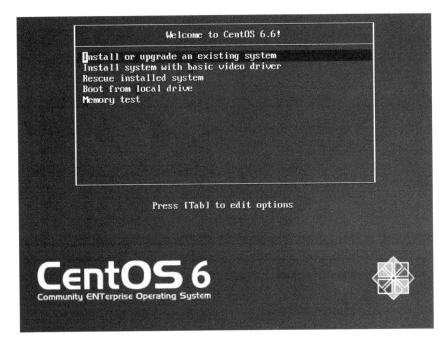

Several scary messages later (all of which are perfectly normal), you may see a screen that offers to verify the installation medium you're using. If you have the time, feel free to verify it - otherwise select skip to continue.

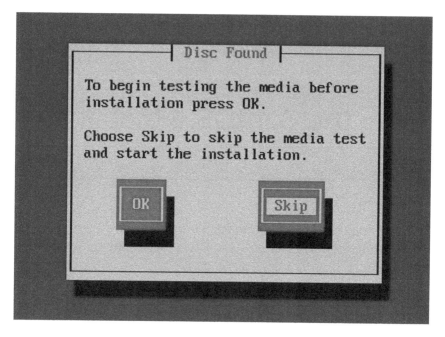

The next screen will only show the CentOS 6 Logo without any information - except for the very easy to overlook **Next** button at the bottom right.

Choose a language and keyboard layout, after which you will be prompted to use either "Basic" or "Specialised Storage Devices". Choose Basic and continue - you can setup specialised equipment later if you have any (in which case, you probably know how to install it better than I do).

You will soon arrive at a screen asking you to identify your computer. A pre-populated text field reads "localhost.localdomain". This is the default name for a Linux system and very non-descriptive. Feel free to change this to something more unique. Short and snappy works best, and all lowercase is appropriate here.

I recommend to use the same description as you may use for an internal domain as discussed in the previous chapter.

 Please name this computer. The hostname identifies the computer on a network.

Hostname: localhost.localdomain

On the same screen, innocently hiding at the bottom left, you'll find a button that reads "Configure Network".

If you're connecting your server with an Ethernet cable, it is vital that you press this button, otherwise CentOS will not connect to your network going forward and you're faced with the impossible task of connecting manually.

Please skip this step if you are connecting to a wireless network.

A list of network interfaces appears. Select the one you want to connect with, click Edit and tick both boxes here: "Connect automatically" and "Available to all users". Select Apply, followed by Close to return to the previous screen.

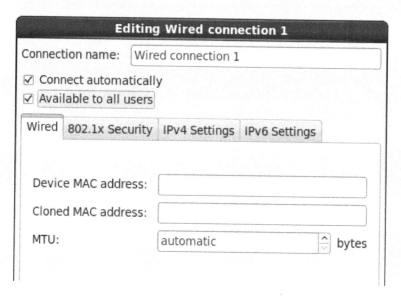

You do not need to do this if you are connecting to a wireless network. Even though wireless connections will show up in the list, the CentOS 6 installer does not provide an option to enter a password for encrypted connections. We will let GNOME make the wireless connection later.

When you're ready, click Next to select your current time zone.

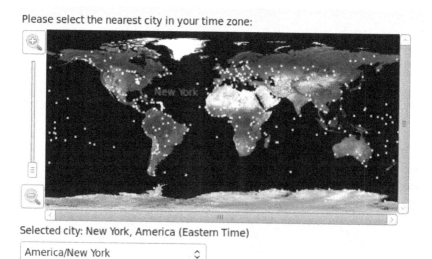

Time to provide a password for the root user. The same principles apply as I mentioned <u>in the CentOS 7 section</u>. If your password isn't strong enough for CentOS, a warning message will appear.

On the next screen, CentOS will ask you what type of installation you would like on your server. I recommend to choose the first option called **"Use all space"**. This will format your drive and delete any data that is currently on your system.

I do not recommend the default option "Replace existing Linux system" as it will not remove any old Windows or Mac installations automatically.

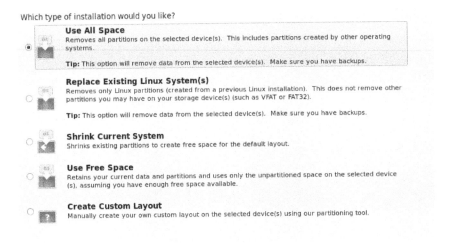

Hit Next to continue and you will be asked if it's OK to "Write the changes to disk". Confirm this and CentOS will go ahead with the installation: it will format your hard drive and use all available space available for the operating system.

The minimal ISO will start to install right away, but the Full DVD ISO will ask you what type of installation you prefer. **Desktop** is the default (the first option) and I recommend we use it. This will install GNOME and allow us to use the server with a graphical user interface that looks like a cross between Windows and macOS.

Depending on the speed of your system this can take some time. Grab a coffee and relax while your computer is hard at work.

The default installation of CentOS is a minimum install. You can optionally select a different set of software now.

- ◉ Desktop
- ○ Minimal Desktop
- ○ Minimal
- ○ Basic Server
- ○ Database Server
- ○ Web Server
- ○ Virtual Host
- ○ Software Development Workstation

When the installer has finished it will ask you to restart your system.

When CentOS starts in Desktop Mode for the first time, it wants you to create a new user for yourself. Do this when prompted. Click Forward on the bottom right hand side when you're done.

Create User

You must create a 'username' for regular (non-administrative) use of your system. To create a system 'username', please provide the information requested below.

Username: [   ]

Full Name: [   ]

Password: [   ]

Confirm Password: [   ]

If you need to use network authentication, such as Kerberos or NIS, please click the Use Network Login button.

On the next screen, choose to **synchronise the time over the internet** and select one of the NTP servers. This service will take affect as soon as we have an internet connection to synchronise the time with.

Date and Time

Please set the date and time for the system.

Date and Time

Current date and time: Tue 03 Mar 2015 01:17:53 PM EST

☑ Synchronize date and time over the network

Synchronize date and time on your computer with a remote time server using the Network Time Protocol:

NTP Servers

0.centos.pool.ntp.org
1.centos.pool.ntp.org
2.centos.pool.ntp.org
3.centos.pool.ntp.org

▷ Advanced Options

The next decision you'll have to make is about something called **Kdump**. It's an automated crash report system designed to capture information in the event of a system crash. Kdump will send valuable information to the developers of the Linux Kernel that may prevent such a crash in the future.

It does require some memory, so if you have less than 2GB available I would recommend not to use it. Simply untick the box (or leave it ticked if you feel so inclined) and click Finish on the bottom right.

Kdump

Kdump is a kernel crash dumping mechanism. In the event of a system crash, kdump will capture information from your system that can be invaluable in determining the cause of the crash. Note that kdump does require reserving a portion of system memory that will be unavailable for other uses.

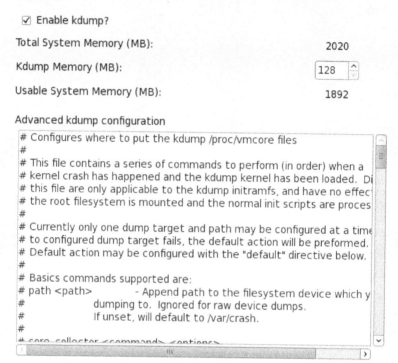

☑ Enable kdump?

Total System Memory (MB):   2020

Kdump Memory (MB):   128

Usable System Memory (MB):   1892

Advanced kdump configuration

```
# Configures where to put the kdump /proc/vmcore files
#
# This file contains a series of commands to perform (in order) when a
# kernel crash has happened and the kdump kernel has been loaded. Di
# this file are only applicable to the kdump initramfs, and have no effec
# the root filesystem is mounted and the normal init scripts are proces
#
# Currently only one dump target and path may be configured at a time
# to configured dump target fails, the default action will be preformed.
# Default action may be configured with the "default" directive below.
#
# Basics commands supported are:
# path <path>        - Append path to the filesystem device which y
#                dumping to.  Ignored for raw device dumps.
#                If unset, will default to /var/crash.
#
# core collector <command> <options>
```

Your system will request a restart one last time, after which the installation is officially finished.

Congratulations, you've just installed CentOS 6!

Logging in to GNOME

When your system has restarted it will automatically boot into GNOME instead of the command line interface.

You will be prompted to login with your credentials here: simply click on your name and enter your password - the one you've set during the installation (not the root password, the other one).

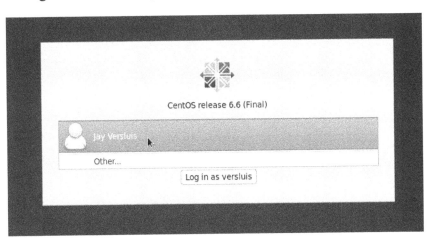

In case you've not worked with GNOME before, it's similar to the relationship that "Windows and DOS" shared in the early years of Windows: GNOME is a graphical user interface for (mostly) command line tools. Much of what can be done on the command line can also be done in GNOME; some tasks are easier to achieve in GNOME, while others are easier to accomplish on the command line.

You can think of GNOME and the command line as two ways to communicate with the operating system.

Note that GNOME is not the only GUI you can install in CentOS: due to the open nature of Linux, more than one such project exists for the various distributions. Other notable GUIs include KDE, Cinnamon, XFCE and MATE. We'll stick with GNOME for now and won't worry about any of the others.

If you ever want to logon to GNOME as root, select "Other..." from the above screen and type in root and its password.

Connecting to your Wireless Network .

Welcome to GNOME! Once you're logged in you should see the Desktop environment, featuring a very deep and dark blue background.

Feel free to explore the features it provides. For our server setup we won't be spending much time with the interface, just know that there's a whole new world waiting for you here.

On the top right hand side, have a look for the **network icon**. It's the small double-screen like icon with the red x symbol at the bottom. It indicates that we currently have no active network connection. When you click this icon, a fly-out menu appears showing available wireless networks in the vicinity:

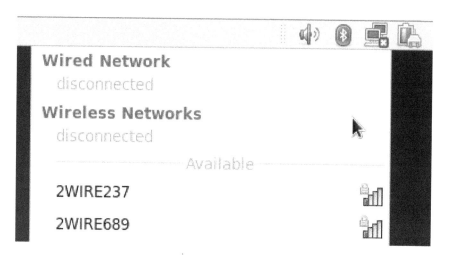

Find your own network in the list and click on it. GNOME will ask for your wireless password, and a few moments later you are connected. The network icon will animate briefly and eventually turn into a "wireless status" icon, resembling a signal strength indicator.

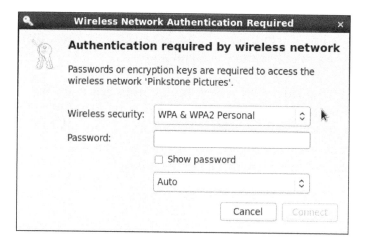

The connection will be established as soon as this user will login again, but it won't be valid for other users by default - including the all important root user. To make it happen, **right-click** on the network/wireless icon and select **"Edit Connections"**.

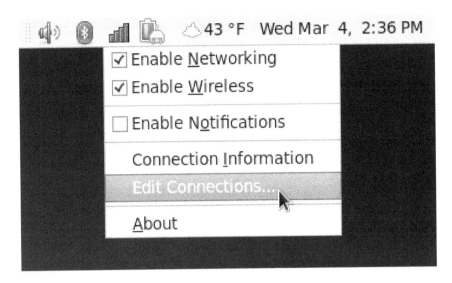

Pick your network from the list and click the **Edit Button** on the right hand side.

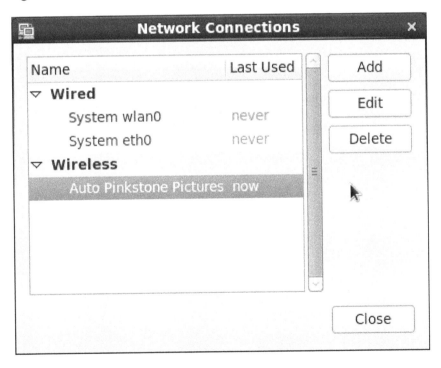

This will bring up another window. All we have to do here is tick the check box that reads **Available to all users** which will do just what we want: make our wireless connection available to other users on this system, including root. As a result, when we restart the system remotely (and consequently not login to GNOME), our server will be reachable on the local network.

Once ticked, select Apply at the bottom of the window.

Finding your IP address in GNOME

While we are dealing with network connections, let's take a look at your server's IP address so you can talk to it from other machines via SSH.

Right-click the network icon (the little bar indicator, just like before) and select **Connection Information**. This will bring up a window similar to the one below. You can find your IP address in the **IPv4 section**:

Connection Information

 ## Active Network Connections

System eth0 (default)

General

Interface:	Ethernet (eth0)
Hardware Address:	00:1C:42:59:28:A2
Driver:	virtio_net
Speed:	Unknown
Security:	None

IPv4

IP Address:	10.211.55.24
Broadcast Address:	10.211.55.255
Subnet Mask:	255.255.255.0
Default Route:	10.211.55.1
Primary DNS:	10.211.55.1

IPv6

Ignored

Close

Disabling laptop suspension when the lid closes

If you're using a laptop as your server (like I do), you'll notice that when you close the lid, your device may go to sleep. That's great when we use our device as a portable laptop in a coffee shop, but it's not so good if our device is to be used as an always-on server system.

The suspension sends our server to sleep and disables our network connection, rendering our LAMP Stack unreachable. Highly undesirable.

Feel free to skip this section if your hardware is not affected by this phenomenon.

To remedy this situation, head over to **System - Preferences - Power Management**.

215

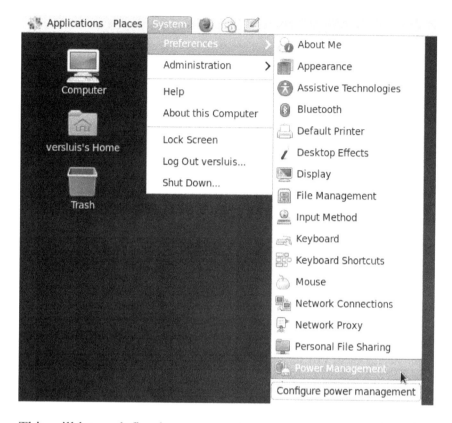

This will let us define how we want our system to react when the lid is closed or the power button is pressed. The first tab is called **"On AC Power"** and it defines values for occasions when your device is plugged in with a charger.

Find the section **"When laptop lid is closed"** and select **Blank Screen** from the drop down menu. This will turn off the display but no longer suspends the system as it does by default.

Make sure to click the **Make Default** button on the bottom. This will prompt for the root password and adopt the settings to all other users on the system.

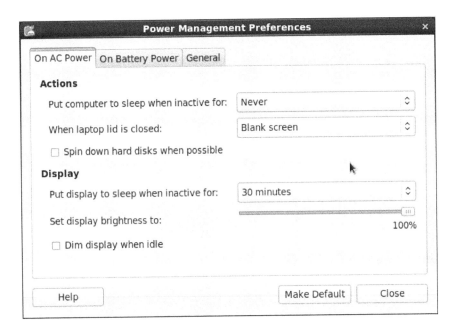

This concludes the necessary steps to enable your wireless connection and enables laptops for remote use. Before restarting the system, make sure you can login via another computer using an SSH client as described in an earlier chapter.

You can now head over to **System - Shutdown** and select **Reboot**. When the system comes back and displays the login screen, simply close the lid and continue adding packages from the command line via SSH.

Installing the LAMP Stack in CentOS 6

The principle of installing Apache and PHP are the same as in CentOS 7, however several principles differ in CentOS 6, for example how to start or stop a service, or how to enable one at boot time.

I will therefore explain the steps necessary to install our LAMP Stack on CentOS 6 in an abbreviated form. For details about why any of these steps are necessary, please refer to the CentOS 7 section.

Let's start with the principle differences.

In CentOS 6 you can start/stop/restart system services using the service command. Note that this command will still work in CentOS 7 and will automatically redirect to its counterpart systemctl (which in turn does not work in CentOS 6).

So the CentOS 6 command

```
service httpd restart
```

is equivalent to the CentOS 7 command

```
systemctl restart httpd.service
```

Likewise, the chkconfig command we use to enable or disable services at boot time still works in CentOS 7 and will also redirect to systemctl.

Therefore, the CentOS 6 command

```
chkconfig httpd on
```

is equivalent to the CentOS 7 command

```
systemctl enable httpd.service
```

Now let's install that LAMP Stack, step by step in CentOS 6:

To install **Apache** (same as in CentOS 7):

```
yum install httpd
```

To start Apache and enable it at boot time:

```
service httpd start
chkconfig httpd on
```

To install **MySQL** (instead of MariaDB):

```
yum install mysql mysql-server
```

To start MySQL and enable it at boot time:

```
service mysql start
chkconfig mysql on
```

To install **PHP** (same as in CentOS 7):

```
yum install php php-mysql php-cli php-gd
```

For PHP to take effect in Apache, let's restart it with

```
service httpd restart
```

That was it for the CentOS 6 installation!

Please follow the steps in the chapter about "Configuring your LAMP Stack".

Extras

In this final chapter I've compiled some tips and tricks for the curious, and for those who want to do even more with their server.

Installing a LAMP Stack on other distributions

If you have tried to apply the instructions for installing the LAMP Stack components on other Linux distributions, you may have noticed that this may not work flawlessly.

Indeed it does not: what we've discussed thus far was unique to CentOS and will most likely work on Fedora, Red Hat Enterprise Linux and Scientific Linux too - although I have not verified this.

When I was discussing an early draft of this book with some of my geek friends, they suggested I should include at least the basic principles of how to get the LAMP Stack going on Debian and Ubuntu. And I agree: both Debian and Ubuntu are two of the most popular distributions in use today.

While I won't be able to cover the installation process for either of these distributions here, I can explain how to install the necessary components – just like I did with CentOS.

The reason why the CentOS commands will not work in Debian and Ubuntu is that the package manager for these distributions greatly differs from yum. Even though the source code used for all distributions is the same, the compiled packages have different names.

For example, the Apache package is called **httpd** in CentOS, but it's called **apache2** in Debian and Ubuntu. Besides, the system services and operating systems work very differently and therefore require different commands.

The next two chapters will get you started building a LAMP Stack on Debian and Ubuntu.

Installing a LAMP Stack on Debian

Debian is available for a variety of architectures, including ARMv7. This makes Debian an ideal candidate for installations on non-PC hardware, such as Android tablets and Chromebooks.

For our purposes I would recommend the small installation image, or netinstall image. You can download these versions here:

- https://www.debian.org/distrib/

New versions of Debian are released every two years, and receive support for an additional year after a new version is released. At the time of writing, the current release is Debian 7 "Wheezy", with Debian 8 "Jessie" just around the corner (the releases are named after Toy Story characters).

Note that web application files are stored in a different location than in CentOS or Ubuntu. In Debian, the web root directory is

- **/var/www**

Login as root using your favourite SSH client, and let's get acquainted with the Debian Package Manager **apt**.

224

Before we start, issue the following command to update the cached list of available packages:

```
apt-get update
```

Now let's install **Apache** with the following command:

```
apt-get install apache2
```

This will also start our web server, but it does not enable it when the system boots. To do this, we can make use of the update-rc.d script:

```
update-rc.d apache2 defaults
```

You should now be able to access an Apache Test Page if you navigate to your server's IP address in a web browser. The page will simply read "It works!".

Now we'll add **PHP** with the following packages:

```
apt-get install php5 php5-gd php5-mysql php4-cli
```

To verify that PHP is running, generate a new file in /var/www with the following content:

```
<?php phpinfo(); ?>
```

Open your web browser and navigate to the file using your server's IP, followed by the filename of the above script. For example,

- http://12.34.56.78/info.php

You should see a rather long page with every detail about PHP.

To check if you have PHP as a command line extension, call **php** **–v** to see its version information:

```
php -v
```

```
PHP 5.4.36-0+deb7u3 (cli) (built: Jan  9 2015
08:07:06)
Copyright (c) 1997-2014 The PHP Group
Zend Engine v2.4.0, Copyright (c) 1998-2014 Zend
Technologies
```

Finally, we'll install MySQL – which on Debian and Ubuntu is still MySQL and not MariaDB, at least at the time of writing:

```
apt-get install mysql-server
```

During the installation you have the opportunity to provide a MySQL root password. When finished, secure the installation using

```
/usr/bin/mysql_secure_installation
```

The procedure from here onwards is the same as described in the CentOS section of this book.

Installing a LAMP Stack on Ubuntu

Package management and the installation of our LAMP components is identical to the Debian instructions. Please refer to the previous chapter to build your LAMP Stack.

Ubuntu itself however has several key differences I'd like to make you aware of.

To begin with, Ubuntu has several types of downloads to offer. For our purposes, choose **Ubuntu Server**. This is a smaller ISO and does not install the desktop environment. You can download it from here:

- http://www.ubuntu.com/download/server

A new version of Ubuntu is released approximately every 6 months with support for roughly two years, except for LTS versions, which have "long term support" for 5 years.

I strongly recommend installing the LTS version for your server project. At the time of writing this is Ubuntu Server 14.04 .2 LTS.

The web root directory in Ubuntu is /var/www/html – just like in CentOS, but unlike in Debian.

Ubuntu does not allow root logins. The root user exists, but for security purposes cannot be used to login to the server via SSH by default, nor will you be asked to create a root password during the installation.

Instead you must login with your standard user and make extensive use of the **sudo** prefix to execute administrative tasks, such as installing packages or editing system wide configuration files.

Prefixing much of what we do with sudo can become a little tiresome, and thankfully there is a way to become root for the duration of your session by issuing the following command:

```
sudo -i
```

The command prompt will change, indicating that you are now root@yourserver.

For more information about using Ubuntu as root, please consult the extensive documentation:

- https://help.ubuntu.com/community/RootSudo.

Ubuntu has a firewall activated by default, much like CentOS. It can be accessed and configured with the **ufw** command, which stands for Uncomplicated Fire Wall.

Before you install packages and access your server from a web browser, you'll have to open port 80 so that web traffic won't be blocked by the firewall.

To open a port, issue this:

```
ufw allow 80
```

Likewise, if you'd like to close a port, issue this:

```
ufw deny 3306
```

You can switch the entire firewall off (and back on again) using these commands:

```
ufw disable
ufw enable
```

Both of these commands will make the change immediately, and also add your preference at boot time: changes to the firewall service will persist if you reboot your server. What a nice touch!

For more information about the Ubuntu Firewall check out the extensive documentation:

- https://help.ubuntu.com/12.04/serverguide/firewall.html.

Transferring an ISO image to USB on macOS

Follow these instructions to copy an ISO image to a USB stick, which will create an installation medium on macOS and Linux. This is a command line operation, so have your Terminal session open to proceed.

The command we need to use for this operation is called **dd** and it can transfer the image to a USB stick for us. The tool needs a few parameters though, so first we'll need to look at how to find those.

To begin with, insert your USB stick and open the **Terminal** utility. You can find it under Applications/Utilities or do a Spotlight search. You should see a command line tool with a cursor, excitedly awaiting some text input. It'll look something like this:

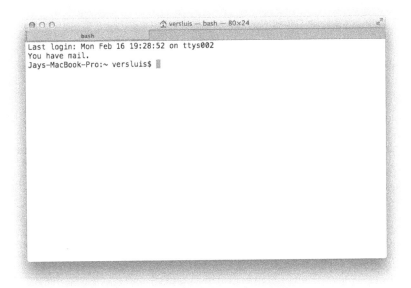

```
Last login: Mon Feb 16 19:28:52 on ttys002
You have mail.
Jays-MacBook-Pro:~ versluis$
```

I'm assuming that your downloaded image file is called centos.iso
and that it resides in your Downloads directory. In reality it will
probably have a slightly more complicated name, such as
"CentOS-6.6-i386-bin-DVD1.iso". Feel free to type it out, or
rename the download to centos.iso. You can even drag it into the
Terminal session from a Finder window.

Let's start by entering your Downloads directory. Issue the
following commands:

```
cd ~/Downloads
ls
```

The first command means "change directory", followed by where
to change into. The tilde symbol (~) is your home directory, and
we're appending /Downloads. It's the equivalent of visiting your
Downloads directory in Finder. The second command lists all
files, and your ISO image should be one of them.

Now that we're in the right location, let's find out what your USB
stick is known as under the hood. The dd command needs to know
which file you want to copy (we know that), as well as the **device**

231

corresponding to your USB stick. It's easy to get confused at this point. Let me explain:

Devices in Linux (and macOS) are things attached to the system, such as hard disk, memory cards and USB sticks. Each device can hold a number of partitions which is where your data is stored.

Depending on how many storage devices are attached to your system, you'll get a specific address for each device. For example, /dev/disk0 is your internal Mac hard disk in which you'll find several partitions (such as /dev/disk0s1).

Since our ISO image will overwrite all partitions on the USB stick, we need to know what our USB stick is "known as" to the system. Type the following to get a list of what's attached where:

```
diskutil list

/dev/disk0
   #:                       TYPE NAME
SIZE         IDENTIFIER
   0:        GUID_partition_scheme
*1.0 TB       disk0
   1:                        EFI EFI
209.7 MB     disk0s1
   2:                  Apple_HFS Macintosh HD
999.3 GB     disk0s2
   3:                  Apple_Boot Recovery HD
650.0 MB     disk0s3
/dev/disk1
   #:                       TYPE NAME
SIZE         IDENTIFIER
   0:        GUID_partition_scheme
*512.1 GB     disk1
   1:                        EFI EFI
209.7 MB     disk1s1
```

```
   2:                        Apple_HFS Macintosh SSD
511.3 GB    disk1s2
   3:                        Apple_Boot Recovery HD
650.0 MB    disk1s3
/dev/disk2
   #:                        TYPE NAME
SIZE          IDENTIFIER
   0:       FDisk_partition_scheme
*1.0 TB      disk2
   1:                        Apple_HFS VM Drive
1.0 TB       disk2s1
/dev/disk3
   #:                        TYPE NAME
SIZE          IDENTIFIER
   0:       GUID_partition_scheme
*1.5 TB      disk3
   1:                        EFI EFI
209.7 MB    disk3s1
   2:                        Apple_HFS Black Time
Machine         1.5 TB      disk3s2
/dev/disk4
   #:                        TYPE NAME
SIZE          IDENTIFIER
   0:       FDisk_partition_scheme
*4.0 GB      disk4
   1:                        DOS_FAT_32 C64
```

Looks like I've got 5 storage devices on my system. The one at the bottom is my USB stick, an old 4GB model currently formatted with FAT32. Your layout will be different, so keep an eye on the SIZE parameter. If your currently formatted stick is named you can identify it that way too (mine is called C64).

The device I want to use here is /dev/disk4. Note that when we get to work, everything on your USB stick will be erased when we copy the ISO over. The dd command will not warn you before this happens.

Before we can continue we need to make sure that your USB stick is not mounted to OS X. When you Mac sees a file system it can read, an orange icon appears on your Desktop. This means the drive is mounted. But since the dd command will do a low level format with a different file system, OS X needs to let go of our stick. If we don't do this, you'll get a "Resource busy" message in the next step.

To unmount your stick, type the following:

```
diskutil unmountDisk /dev/disk4

Unmount of all volumes on disk4 was successful
```

That orange icon should disappear from the desktop, and you will no longer see your USB stick in the Finder either. Leave it attached though – do not eject it.

Now let's give our cryptic dd command something to do. Since we're in the correct directory already, type the following (you will be prompted for your computer password):

```
sudo dd if=centos.iso of=/dev/disk4 bs=4m

// time passes...
694272+0 records in
694272+0 records out
355467264 bytes transferred in 249.100402 secs
    (1427004 bytes/sec)
```

Amend /dev/disk4 with your own device. Feel free to specify the direct path to your image file in place of centos.iso (you cannot use wildcards I'm afraid, but you can drag a file from a Finder window directly into the Terminal session, resulting in the path to the file).

Writing a disk image to USB this way can take a long while, during which time you won't get any feedback whatsoever. That's normal, even though it looks like your session hangs. If your USB stick has a light you'll be able to see it flashing - but you're in the dark about the progress (literally).

Feel free to do other things with your Mac, as long as you leave the Terminal window open. Eventually you'll see a message like the above, telling you how long it took and how many bytes were copied.

I was copying a 190MB image and it took just over four minutes. That's because I had an abysmally slow USB stick – something to keep in mind when you want to transfer a large ISO image onto a stick from 10 years ago. You're not doing yourself a favour: it'll take hours to copy, and just as long to boot from later on.

Should you want to terminate your dd session (perhaps to use a faster USB stick), simply hit **CTRL+C** and you'll be returned to the command line.

If all went well you'll receive a summary message at the end. Now you're ready to boot from your stick into the wonderful world of CentOS.

How do I find my IP Address?

If you're logged in as root on the command line, you can run **ip addr show**. This will output the IP addresses of all connected network interfaces.

Below is an example of a laptop connected to the network via Wi-Fi:

```
ip addr show
```

```
1: lo: <LOOPBACK,UP,LOWER_UP> mtu 65536 qdisc
noqueue state UNKNOWN
    link/loopback 00:00:00:00:00:00 brd
00:00:00:00:00:00
    inet 127.0.0.1/8 scope host lo
    inet6 ::1/128 scope host
      valid_lft forever preferred_lft forever
2: wlan0: <BROADCAST,MULTICAST,UP,LOWER_UP> mtu
1500 qdisc mq state UP qlen 1000
    link/ether 00:24:2b:2e:0f:a4 brd
ff:ff:ff:ff:ff:ff
    inet 10.0.1.73/24 brd 10.0.1.255 scope
global wlan0
    inet6 fe80::224:2bff:fe2e:fa4/64 scope link
      valid_lft forever preferred_lft forever
```

```
3: eth0: <NO-CARRIER,BROADCAST,MULTICAST,UP> mtu
1500 qdisc pfifo_fast state DOWN qlen 1000
    link/ether 00:13:77:d4:da:d0 brd
ff:ff:ff:ff:ff:ff
```

This system shows a total of three interfaces: the first one is the loopback interface we've briefly talked about earlier. It's for local testing only, so 127.0.0.1 is not our IP address.

The second interface is the wireless LAN on which this machine is connected. Notice the line beginning with **inet**: that's our IP address! See the /24 at the end of that IP? This is the subnet in which the IP resides (/24 stands for subnet 255.255.255.0). The full IP here is **10.0.1.73**.

The third interface is a wired LAN interface. It's enabled but unconnected – hence it shows no IP address here.

Note that if you are not logged in as root, the ip command cannot be found due to the way the shell is setup: standard users do not have the location of the command in their path variable by default. But fear not: we can still run the command by specifying the full path, like so:

```
/sbin/ip addr show
```

It works on all major distributions of Linux.

How do I verify the downloaded image file?

When you've downloaded the ISO file for your distribution, it is considered good practice to check if the file is fit for use. It allows us to check if the download was successful, preventing unwanted surprises.

Together with the ISO images, distribution providers release several checksum files that are commonly found in the same directory as the binary files from which we create our installation media. Three flavours are currently in use:

- MD5
- SHA or SHA1
- SHA256

These are tools with which a checksum (sometimes called "hash values") can be generated with varying degrees of accuracy. The idea behind a checksum is that it will be different depending on what data is present in the file: a small change to the file – typically from a download error – would result in a different checksum.

Let's take CentOS 7 and MD5 as an example.

In the directory from which you've downloaded your ISO image, there should be a file called md5sum.txt. Open it to see something like this:

```
713ea7847adcdd1700e92429f212721a  CentOS-7.0-
1406-x86_64-DVD.iso
39179ca247b95a4adfcc4ecee3f4605d  CentOS-7.0-
1406-x86_64-Everything.iso
099b7cfe761d1ecd7d23eaecfef1a44c  CentOS-7.0-
1406-x86_64-GnomeLive.iso
b7188b1632b5494c6bf458f744cadbfa  CentOS-7.0-
1406-x86_64-KdeLive.iso
3389283dc715ee65e15ef06d9e335acb  CentOS-7.0-
1406-x86_64-livecd.iso
96de4f38a2f07da51831153549c8bd0c  CentOS-7.0-
1406-x86_64-NetInstall.iso
e3afe3f1121d69c40cc23f0bafa05e5d  CentOS-7.0-
1406-x86_64-Minimal.iso
```

That long number at the beginning of each line is the MD5 checksum for the file at the end of each line. SHA1 and SHA256 will have similar files in the same directory.

Say you had downloaded the "minimal" ISO file, you can run a command against your downloaded copy of the file and create your own checksum. Then you can compare it to the one listed in the directory.

The procedure is different for every operating system and every hash flavour.

Windows

Microsoft provide a small command line utility called "File Checksum Integrity Verifier" from the following URL:

- http://www.microsoft.com/en-us/download/details.aspx?id=11533

Once downloaded, extract it into your Downloads directory. A small file called fciv.exe will now be available to you from the Windows Command Prompt. Open it to see another black scary window which looks similar to our SSH client. You can find it under All Programs - Accessories.

Navigate to your Downloads folder by typing

```
cd Downloads
```

I'm assuming that your ISO file also resides in this folder and is called centos.iso. In reality it's probably something much longer like "CentOS-7.0-1406-x86_64-Minimal.iso".

Now use the fciv command, followed by your filename:

```
fciv centos.iso

//
// File Checksum Integrity Verifier version
2.05.
//
e3afe3f1121d69c40cc23f0bafa05e5d  centos.iso
```

The command will take some time to make its calculations: the bigger the file, and the slower your computer, the longer the wait. With some luck, the MD5 checksum will match the one in the download directory.

macOS

On your Mac you can use the md5 command inside a Terminal session to verify your downloads.

As above, I'm assuming that your file is called centos.iso and that it resides inside your Downloads directory. Call md5 with the filename as the only parameter:

```
md5 ~/Downloads/centos.iso

MD5 (centos.iso) =
96de4f38a2f07da51831153549c8bd0c
```

Linux

Most distributions include the **openssl** command with which we can create an MD5 checksum from a file. Here's how:

```
openssl md5 centos.iso

MD5(centos.iso)=
96de4f38a2f07da51831153549c8bd0c
```

This approach also works on macOS.

How do I increase the file upload limit in PHP?

Web applications allow us to upload files via web server. Those files are stored inside the web root directory, and the upload procedures are typically called via PHP scripts.

By default, PHP limits the amount of data we can upload to 2MB – not very much by today's standards: casual video files may easily exceed 100MB.

To remedy this we have two options: tweak this setting system wide by editing the **php.ini** file, or amend the **.htaccess** file in our web root directory.

To edit the php.ini file:

From the command line, logged in as root, open a vi session to edit /etc/php.ini like so:

```
vi /etc/php.ini
```

Find a section called **File Uploads** in which you should find the following text:

```
; Maximum allowed size for uploaded files.
;
http://www.php.net/manual/en/ini.core.php#ini.up
load-max-filesize
upload_max_filesize = 2M
```

Replace 2M in the last line with something more suitable, perhaps 512M.

To edit your .htaccess file:

I'm assuming that your web application resides in the web root directory. If you have multiple apps installed in subfolders, tweak the path accordingly. Open a vi session and edit .htaccess like this:

```
vi /var/www/html/.htaccess
```

At the bottom of the file, add the following line:

```
php_value upload_max_filesize 512M
```

Feel free to amend 512M with the value of your choice. Your changes will be in effect immediately.

How do I increase the memory limit in PHP?

PHP scripts are allowed to use a certain portion of memory during execution. On CentOS the default value is set to 128MB. This is often sufficient to run fairly complex web applications.

However, if your particular web app is giving you grief about this, you'll be pleased to hear that you can change this easily, with a choice of two approaches:

The first option is to change the memory limit defined in the **php.ini** file. In the **Resource Limits** section, find the following lines:

```
; Maximum amount of memory a script may consume
(128MB)
;
http://www.php.net/manual/en/ini.core.php#ini.me
mory-limit
memory_limit = 128M
```

Change 128M to something higher (512M, 1G, etc) or lower if you're running out of memory.

Alternatively, you can edit your web application's .htaccess file. This will also let you define a higher (or lower) memory limit. You will typically find it in the web root directory, or a subfolder if you have more than one web application installed.

Add the following line to the bottom of **/var/www/html/.htaccess**:

```
php_value memory_limit 128M
```

Replace 128M with your desired memory limit. Your changes should be effective immediately.

How do I boot my server in Rescue Mode?

There may come the time when we cannot boot our server anymore, be that through a hardware failure or a configuration problem.

One of the most common scenarios is that we make a mistake when editing a system wide configuration file, try to restart the system and realize that nothing seems to work anymore.

It's easy to undo such mistakes – if we find a way to start the server from an external drive.

You'll be pleased to hear that your installation medium comes with an option to boot into **Rescue Mode**. This will start CentOS from your external drive, be that a USB stick or DVD, and let you change files that may cause problems.

Note that this procedure is designed for emergencies only, or for operations that require our regular installation to be dormant. In this chapter I will show you how to boot into Rescue Mode.

Shut off your server and start it up from the installation medium. You should see the familiar start-up screen:

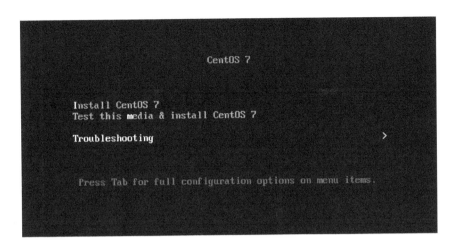

Select **Troubleshooting**, and on the next screen, choose **Rescue a CentOS System**.

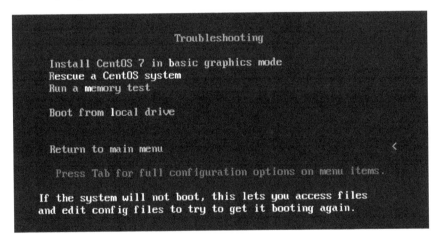

CentOS will not start from your hard disk and instead offer to mount your regular system so that you can make changes and rectify mistakes.

The next screen will provide you with several options on how to proceed: select **Continue** to mount your regular installation with read/write access. You can also choose to skip this step entirely, or mount it with read-only privileges. Neither of these options will let you make changes though.

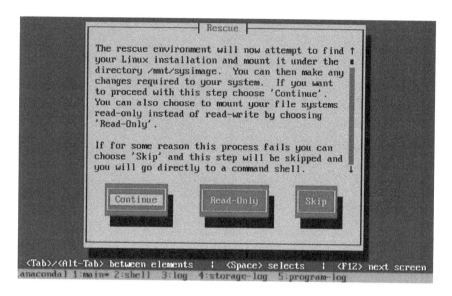

The rescue system will tell you that your hard disk installation has been mounted at **/mnt/sysimage**. This means that what used to be accessible via / (the server's root directory) is now accessible at /mnt/sysimage.

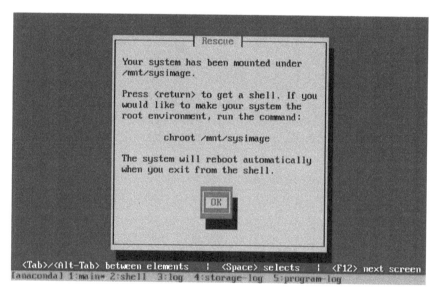

You will receive another tip that may require a little more explanation: how to make your hard disk installation become the root environment. Here's what this means:

When you've used your Linux system for a while, you get used to the location of things. For example, your web root directory is at

- /var/www/html

But with the rescue system, technically your web root directory is at

- /mnt/sysimage/var/www/html

That's just very tough to type and can easily lead to mistakes. It's the last thing we need when we're under pressure!

So instead, you can "change root" and make your regular hard disk image the new root environment, courtesy of the **chroot** command. It will simply change what the shell sees as the start of your path.

Let's try it out:

```
chroot /mnt/sysimage
```

As soon as you've changed root, all your files and locations are accessible again as if you're operating on the real system. Before the change, a command like

```
ls /var/www/html
```

would have certainly produced an error. After the change you can use it without problems.

Now you can start troubleshooting and try to restart your system again from your hard drive.

You can learn more about the chroot command by reading its man page.

Feel free to visit the CentOS Documentation for a more detailed explanation of the entire rescue procedure:

- https://www.centos.org/docs/5/html/Installation_Guide-en-US/s1-rescuemode-boot.html

How to leave Rescue Mode

While I can't help you with the actual troubleshooting procedure, I can tell you how to get out of rescue mode and back into your real CentOS installation.

Use the **exit** command.

If you have chrooted your previous installation, you must issue the command twice: once to leave the chroot environment, and then again to leave the rescue system.

CentOS will try to boot into your regular system again automatically. Make sure to remove the installation medium; otherwise you'll start the installer again (which is probably not what you want).

How to format a disk drive in Linux

As I promised earlier, in this chapter I will explain how to format a new device in Linux with the file system of your choice.

If you are used to GUI based formatting tools, such as Mac's Disk Utility or Windows Disk Management, then the Linux procedure may look a little complex at first.

It's all about knowing why we need to do what, and then appreciating how much a GUI tool does for us.

To make use of a new device, four steps are necessary:

- find out what device our drive is "known as" to Linux
- create a new partition
- format the partition with a file system
- mount the partition to a directory

Let's see how this works step by step.

What's my device called?

The **fdisk** command will let us see a list of currently available devices on our system:

```
fdisk -l
```

The output will vary depending on how many devices are attached to your system:

```
Disk /dev/sda: 68.7 GB, 68719476736 bytes,
134217728 sectors
Units = sectors of 1 * 512 = 512 bytes
Sector size (logical/physical): 512 bytes / 4096
bytes
I/O size (minimum/optimal): 4096 bytes / 4096
bytes
Disk label type: dos
Disk identifier: 0x000641ba
    Device Boot      Start            End
Blocks    Id   System
/dev/sda1    *          2048      1026047
512000    83   Linux
/dev/sda2           1026048    134217727
66595840    8e   Linux LVM
Disk /dev/sdb: 68.7 GB, 68719476736 bytes,
134217728 sectors
Units = sectors of 1 * 512 = 512 bytes
Sector size (logical/physical): 512 bytes / 4096
bytes
I/O size (minimum/optimal): 4096 bytes / 4096
bytes
Disk label type: dos
Disk identifier: 0xfaa25abe
    Device Boot      Start            End
Blocks   Id   System
```

```
/dev/sdb1              2048    134217727
67107840   83  Linux
Disk /dev/sdc: 68.7 GB, 68719476736 bytes,
134217728 sectors
Units = sectors of 1 * 512 = 512 bytes
Sector size (logical/physical): 512 bytes / 4096
bytes
I/O size (minimum/optimal): 4096 bytes / 4096
bytes
```

Such output looks more scary than it really is, let me break it down for clarity. The above system with three drives:

- /dev/sda
- /dev/sdb
- /dev/sdc

We can see this by the line starting with Disk, followed by the device name, followed by the size of the device. Let's take a look at /dev/sdb:

```
Disk /dev/sdb: 68.7 GB, 68719476736 bytes,
134217728 sectors
Units = sectors of 1 * 512 = 512 bytes
Sector size (logical/physical): 512 bytes / 4096
bytes
```

If any partitions are present, fdisk will list those too, underneath the device information:

```
Device Boot      Start        End      Blocks
Id  System
/dev/sdb1              2048    134217727
67107840   83  Linux
```

We can see this under the indented heading that starts with Device. In our example we have a single partition on /dev/sdb, namely

254

/dev/sdb1. If a file system can be identified, fdisk will show us this too.

Take a look at /dev/sdc: the device is present but does not currently hold a partition. Let's add one now.

Creating a new partition with fdisk

I'm assuming that we want to create a single partition using all available space on our device. That's usually the best for portable drives such as SD cards and USB sticks.

Issue the **fdisk** command, followed by the device you'd like to partition. In our case that's /dev/sdc:

```
fdisk /dev/sdc
```

fdisk will now launch as a wizard like tool, awaiting your input as one-letter characters. Press m to see a list of all commands you can issue.

The list tells us that with p we will be shown a list of partitions on the device. We're not expecting anything, so let's test that theory:

```
p

Disk /dev/sdc: 68.7 GB, 68719476736 bytes,
134217728 sectors
Units = sectors of 1 * 512 = 512 bytes
Sector size (logical/physical): 512 bytes / 4096
bytes
I/O size (minimum/optimal): 4096 bytes / 4096
bytes
Disk label type: dos
```

```
Disk identifier: 0x1a97134f
   Device Boot       Start           End
Blocks    Id  System
```

Nothing, as expected – otherwise we'd see some output underneath the last line, just like we did when we issued fdisk –l.

We need to create at least a single partition, so let's press n.

```
Command (m for help): n

Partition type:
   p   primary (0 primary, 0 extended, 4 free)
   e   extended
Select (default p):
```

We must now choose to create a Primary or an Extended partition. Since we're only interested in a single partition, let's make it primary and press p. Doing so means that we need to specify which of the four possible primary partitions we are creating, so we'll select 1.

Next we need to tell fdisk how much space we'd like to use. Press enter to accept the defaults, which are set to the maximum available space on the device:

```
Partition number (1-4, default 1): 1
First sector (2048-134217727, default 2048):
Using default value 2048
Last sector, +sectors or +size{K,M,G} (2048-
134217727, default 134217727):
Using default value 134217727
Partition 1 of type Linux and of size 64 GiB is
set
```

Excellent! The final step is to write all these changes to disk. Press m if you can't remember which letter to press, or trust me when I tell you it's w:

```
The partition table has been altered!
Calling ioctl() to re-read partition table.
Syncing disks.
```

Creating a file system on the new partition

With the partition in place, we need to format it so that data can be stored inside it. Linux has a variety of file systems to offer and it's up to us to specify which one we want to use. I'm going to choose EXT4 for my new hard disk, a very robust native Linux file system.

If I wanted to format a portable drive, like a USB Stick or SD Card, I'd probably choose FAT32 so I can read it on other (non-Linux) systems too. More on this in a moment.

We can use the mkfs command to create a file system:

```
mkfs -t ext4 /dev/sdc1
```

```
mke2fs 1.42.9 (28-Dec-2013)
Filesystem label=
OS type: Linux
Block size=4096 (log=2)
Fragment size=4096 (log=2)
Stride=0 blocks, Stripe width=0 blocks
4194304 inodes, 16776960 blocks
838848 blocks (5.00%) reserved for the super
user
First data block=0
Maximum filesystem blocks=2164260864
```

257

```
512 block groups
32768 blocks per group, 32768 fragments per
group
8192 inodes per group
Superblock backups stored on blocks:
     32768, 98304, 163840, 229376, 294912,
819200, 884736, 1605632, 2654208,
     4096000, 7962624, 11239424
Allocating group tables: done
Writing inode tables: done
Creating journal (32768 blocks): done
Writing superblocks and filesystem accounting
information: done
```

Replace the parameter after –t with the file system of your choice (such as ext2, ext3, vfat, ntfs, etc) and specify the partition. Note that /dev/sdc is the device we've partitioned earlier, and /dev/sdc1 is the first partition on the device.

To use file formats that are not native to Linux, such as FAT32, you need to install a package such as **dosfstools** using the package manager for your distribution.

See **man mkfs** for a full list of supported file formats and more usage details.

Mounting the new disk

The last step to make use of our newly formatted device is to mount it somewhere, so that we can access it via the file system.

Two things are necessary for that: we need to create a new (or choose an existing) directory on which to mount the drive, and then mount the partition to that directory.

For this example we'll create a new directory called **/newdrive** and mount our partition there.

```
mkdir /newdrive
mount /dev/sdc1 /newdrive
df -h /newdrive
```

```
Filesystem      Size  Used Avail Use% Mounted on
/dev/sdc1       63G   53M   60G   1% /newdrive
```

The df command can show us how much free space we have available. Not all of our 64GB is usable because of the EXT4 journal and organizational data.

Making the mount permanent

Mounting a drive as shown above will not survive a reboot: If we wanted to mount this drive permanently, we will have to add an entry into the **/etc/fstab** file. Linux reads this file when the system starts and mounts all partitions as specified.

To include our own drive, open a vi session:

```
vi /etc/fstab
```

You will see a list of existing mounts. Simply add your own to the bottom like this:

```
/dev/sdc1 /newdrive ext4    defaults        1 2
```

Here we specify the device, the mount point, our file system, plus three parameters (defaults, 1 and 2), separated by at least one space each. Multiple spaces are allowed for readability.

Without the mysterious three parameters your system may not boot correctly. Omitting or misspelling them means the end of happiness: if your system cannot mount a device as specified,

Linux will boot into emergency mode until you rectify the problem!

Mounting at boot time is not recommended for portable devices: inserting a USB stick into another port for example may result in a different device allocation. To overcome this problem, you can mount known devices using their UUID.

See **man fstab** for more details.

Help! I can't login via SSH – what gives?

Some servers just won't let you login via SSH, and there can be several reasons for it. Follow these instructions if you can ping the server, but if your SSH client gives you an error messages such as "Connection refused".

If you cannot ping the server, or you get an error message such as "Unknown host", your server is very likely not connected to the network you're trying to login from. Make sure to check your network connection before you proceed.

The most common reasons for the "Connection refused" error is:

- no SSH server is installed
- the firewall is blocking connections on port 22
- root is not allowed to login via SSH

To proceed with your investigation, login as root locally at your server's terminal (meaning an attached keyboard and monitor).

To check if an SSH server is installed:

We can use the service command to see if the SSH daemon is running. On CentOS and Fedora it's called **sshd**, on Debian and Ubuntu it's called **ssh**.

The output of the service command will vary between distributions. If the ssh daemon is running, you will receive a positive affirmation such as "it's active" or "it's running". Here's an example from CentOS 7:

```
service sshd status

sshd.service - OpenSSH server daemon
   Loaded: loaded
(/usr/lib/systemd/system/sshd.service; enabled)
   Active: active (running) since Thu 2015-03-12
15:54:01 EDT; 1min 49s ago
  Process: 1539 ExecStartPre=/usr/sbin/sshd-
keygen (code=exited, status=0/SUCCESS)
 Main PID: 1569 (sshd)
   CGroup: /system.slice/sshd.service
           └1569 /usr/sbin/sshd -D
```

Alternatively you may receive a message such as "it's dead", or "inactive" or "unrecognized service". This can either mean that no SSH server is installed, or that the daemon is simply not running. Try starting it first (using "service sshd start", or "service ssh start") and see if this rectifies your problem.

If you're certain that no SSH server is installed, use the relevant package manager to add it to the system. Minimal Debian installations do not come with an SSH server.

On Debian and Ubuntu, use this to install and enable the service:

```
apt-get install openssh-server
```

On CentOS and Fedora, the sshd package is already part of the minimal installation. Just in case it's not there, you can install it with

```
yum install openssh-server
```

You need to start the daemon manually via

```
service sshd start
```

and make sure it starts at boot time too:

```
service sshd on
```

To check if the firewall is blocking ssh connections:

Turn off the firewall temporarily, then try to connect again. If it works, configure the firewall as explained in an earlier chapter (using **system-config-firewall-tui** on CentOS, or using **ufw** on Ubuntu).

On CentOS 7 you can switch off the firewall with this:

```
sytemctl stop firewalld.service
```

On CentOS 6 use this:

```
service iptables stop
```

And on Ubuntu, use this:

```
ufw disable
```

To check if root is allowed to login via SSH:

The SSH daemon can disallow logins from root. Some cloud providers do this to eliminate brute force attacks from evildoers. Users are expected either not to login as root, or use a keyfile instead of a password.

This can be changed in the open-ssh configuration file:

```
vi /etc/ssh/sshd_conf
```

Under "Authentication", find the following line:

```
PermitRootLogin yes
```

If it's set to **yes**, root logins via SSH are allowed. If it's set to **no**, root logins via SSH are disabled. Change appropriately and restart the ssh server.

On CentOS:

```
service sshd restart
```

On Debian and Ubuntu:

```
service ssh restart
```

About the author

Hi, I'm Jay Versluis, and I'm the author here. Nice to meet you, and thank you for reading this book!

I've been writing about web technologies for many years, more for myself than for anybody else. I take notes about things my brain frequently forgets, and over the years I've had many friendly comments by likeminded individuals who have thanked me for such notes. Many were in the same situation as I was: trying to figure out difficult things for which there appears to be no user manual, or the instructions are just too difficult to understand.

Computers are more than just machines to me: they are individuals with whom we can communicate, and each of them has their own little quirks. I don't hold more regard for my coffee maker than for my laptop: they both have benefits, and together they make my life wonderful. I love hardware, software packages and operating systems – but not necessarily in that order.

My history with computers goes back to the mid eighties when everyone at school started playing games on early home computers. The three popular ones at the time were the ZX Spectrum, the Amstrad CPC and the Commodore 64. I was lucky to get my hands on the latter, after convincing my parents that owning one was a life and death situation. I don't think I've ever asked them for anything else.

I loved the Commodore BASIC: it was a major thrill to communicate with a machine in a language both the computer and I could understand. It was like a new life form had been discovered, and I started speaking to it. I still hold the same fascination today when I talk to Linux machines via the command line. I didn't dream that "hacking computers" would be considered a career some years later.

I went online for the first time when my colleague and I both purchased a modem in 1996. Mine was a 19.2k Dr. Neuhaus metal box that only ever connected at 14.4k. I was with CompuServe at the time, and as part of being a customer I was given a generous 2MB of web space. The lengthy URL was soon replaced by my first real domain, which I still own and use today.

Remote computers have always fascinated me, and I often wondered how they work and why they're always ready for requests from web browsers and email clients. It wasn't until 2008 that I rented my first Linux server to take a closer look under the hood.

There seems to be a huge divide between people who know "everything", and those who know "much less" but are eager to learn. I found it extremely tough to get started with the basics.

One reason for writing this book was that this is the guide I wish I had when I started exploring this subject on my own: a kick-start in the right direction, supplementing the various tough to understand articles on the web.

Today I look after various remote servers around the world on behalf of my clients.

By the same author

Online Publications:

- The WP Guru – http://wpguru.co.uk
- iOS Dev Diary – http://pinkstone.co.uk
- Jay's Personal Blog – http://www.versluis.com

Disclaimer

I have written this book in the hope that it will be useful, but cannot give you any guarantee that my instructions will work on every system. I can therefore not be held responsible for potential damage or data loss that occurs as a result of following my instructions.

While I believe the information contained herein to be correct, I am only human – and as such some facts may simply be wrong. There may be better ways to accomplish the things that I have described.

www.ingramcontent.com/pod-product-compliance
Lightning Source LLC
Chambersburg PA
CBHW031236050326
40690CB00007B/831